THE SOCCER GOALKEEPING HANDBOOK

THE SOCCER **GOALKEEPING HANDBOOK** ◼

The essential guide for players and coaches

ALEX WELSH

2nd edition

A&C Black • London
www.acblack.com

Second edition published in 2004 by
A & C Black Publishers Ltd
37 Soho Square, London W1D 3QZ
www.acblack.com

First edition 1998

ISBN 0 7136 6678 1

A CIP catalogue record for this book
is available from the British Library.

Acknowledgements
Cover photograph © Action Images
All other photographs © Empics

A & C Black uses paper produced with elemental
chlorine-free pulp, harvested from managed sustainable forests.

Typeset in 10/11pt Galliard

Printed and bound in Singapore by
Tien Wah Press (Pte) Ltd

Dedication

For Maria, Andrew, John and James

CONTENTS

ACKNOWLEDGEMENTS

I am very pleased to have the opportunity through this second edition, to update the ideas and practices in this book. As the demands of the game are constantly changing it is vital that coaches ensure that their work with players is relevant and keeps pace with current match requirements. After all if coaching does not lead to improved match performance it is pointless.

In producing this book I would like to thank my good friends Pauline Cope (Charlton Athletic Ladies FC), Paul Heald (Wimbledon FC) and Stuart Taylor (Arsenal FC) for their excellent contribution. The photo shoot was great fun and the standard of goalkeeping demonstrated in the impromptu training session at the end was breathtaking. I have coached all three of them at various stages of their careers and they are all tremendous goalkeepers.

I am also indebted to the many specialist coaches I have befriended over the years, in particular Perry Suckling for his ideas, generosity and integrity. My biggest vote of thanks goes to Bob Wilson who has exerted the greatest influence on my coaching career. As one of the world's leading authorities on the art of goalkeeping, Bob has been a tremendous source of knowledge and inspiration and taught me to always accentuate the positive. Thanks also to all the goalkeepers I have coached over the years. Each of them has presented a new challenge and helped me to improve my coaching effectiveness.

Finally, I am extremely grateful to my wife Maria for not only typing the original manuscript and curbing my verbosity but also for her continued support of my coaching work.

The Soccer Goalkeeping Handbook is one of the best ever books written about the art of goalkeeping. It is certainly the most comprehensive. Whether you hold a burning ambition to play 'between the sticks', have a desire to coach and improve aspiring talent, or are simply curious about this most complex position, this is a manual that will broaden your knowledge, surprise you and best of all – inspire you.

Having worked with Alex Welsh over many years, I am flattered to constantly hear myself talking within these pages. We have always shared ideas, thoughts and beliefs. Without sounding conceited, we believe 'our way' should be the benchmark adopted by national governing bodies.

The Soccer Goalkeeping Handbook is based on the best coaching principles and that is why I am so proud to be associated with it. Read this handbook, read it again, absorb it all and then, as a keeper, go out and improve your game or, as a coach, blend the best of these ideals with the best of you.

All you need to know about modern-day goalkeeping is contained within these pages. Simply adapt them to your own style, strengths and personality.

Bob Wilson
Arsenal FC and Scotland
Arsenal FC Head Goalkeeping Coach
Sports Broadcaster

Clockwise from top left: Alex Welsh, Pauline Cope, Stuart Taylor, Paul Heald.

Contrary to the popular theory, goalkeepers are not mad,
they are just a breed apart.

Without doubt, the goalkeeper is the most important position in the soccer team, a view supported by the increasing number of full-time goalkeeping coaches. The performance of the goalkeeper can make or break a team, and it is no coincidence that the most successful clubs have the best keepers. The 'mad' label reflects the individual nature of the job and the lengths to which the keeper will go to protect his goal. Most of the goalkeepers I have met place a clean sheet before personal safety and, therefore, those who do not share the obsession are driven to question their sanity.

This common purpose has led to the development of a genuine camaraderie between goalkeepers. It is often said that they are the keenest of rivals but the best of friends, and this is true. After a match goalkeepers often get together to chat about aspects of their craft in a way that outfield players do not.

Soccer is a team game until the goalkeeper makes a mistake and then it becomes an individual sport.

There is little doubt that the position of goalkeeper is the most pressurised on the field and often the loneliest. All players will make errors, but the keeper's usually result in a goal conceded. Once he manages to keep his mistakes to a minimum and proves his reliability, his work will be measured by the important saves he makes. Good goalkeepers put their mistakes behind them and learn from the experience. One mistake does not make a bad goalkeeper, or one save a good goalkeeper. So what are the factors that make the good goalkeeper stand out from the crowd?

THE QUALITIES OF THE GOALKEEPER

Natural ability

Natural ability is essential, but it needs to be combined with hard work, good coaching and challenging match experience. It is very difficult to define natural ability, but when I see a young goalkeeper for the first time, I look carefully at his handling and footwork skills. The outfield player equivalent of these two aspects is 'touch' (or control) and pace. Handling is the fundamental skill of goalkeeping and without the basic ability to judge the flight of the ball and execute a successful catch, no progress will be made. Similarly, without the capacity to cover the ground quickly to be in the right place at the right time, little will be achieved.

Competitiveness

Good players do not become great without committing themselves wholeheartedly to improving their craft and ultimately their match performance. This inner drive is easy to detect in goalkeepers – how much does he want to prevent the ball going into the net? The extent to which the player does not want to be beaten will determine how hard he will work to polish his strengths and minimise his weaknesses. This, of course, will involve some degree of self-assessment and it is imperative that the keeper is totally honest with himself.

Another characteristic of successful goalkeepers is their ability to cope with the pressure of making mistakes. All keepers make errors but the best have the mental toughness not to let them undermine confidence or to allow one mistake to lead to another.

Soccer intelligence

Since the goalkeeper is expected to play virtually as an additional outfield player, either to patrol the area behind the defence or to initiate attacks, it is essential that he is able to read the game. He should be able to support this understanding with sound decision making. The ability to consistently make good decisions usually distinguishes the confident, positive player from the nervous, unreliable one.

Presence

The truly great goalkeepers appear to have an ability to fill up the goal. They play with such authority and confidence that they inspire those around them. It is important that young goalkeepers learn to develop this on-field personality, a determination to be in control of rather than be controlled by the situation.

GAINING MATCH EXPERIENCE

Appropriate match experience is essential if the goalkeeper is to develop in the right way. Ideally the player should not be performing at a standard where he is too comfortable. If his potential is to be fulfilled, the demands placed on him should be challenging.

This may involve playing promising youngsters above their age group. The coach must remember that actual match practice is the richest learning environment.

THE ROLE OF THE COACH

The perceptive coach will be able to observe his goalkeeper's match performance and isolate areas that require special attention during training. Furthermore, by facing every given situation in training the keeper will be able to recognise it when it happens in a game, and hopefully be able to deal with it. Coaching based on this principle, that is tailored to the individual needs of the goalkeeper, will help him to grow in confidence and competence.

As the game is constantly changing and, with it, the demands placed on players, it is vital that coaches move with the times and meet the challenges of the modern game. No position has changed more radically over the last ten years than the goalkeeper's. *The Soccer Goalkeeping Handbook* will thoroughly examine the goalkeeper's craft and provide advice for players and coaches alike. Each chapter includes an overview of a particular skill or technique with accompanying progressive exercises and coaching points. Throughout, the key to success is the application of sound basic technique and good decision making combined with unshakeable self-belief.

COACHING GOALKEEPERS

If learning is a journey, coaching is the map

Coaches of teams at all levels need to be well equipped to look after their goalkeepers. It has been said that it takes a goalkeeper to coach a goalkeeper and there is some truth in this. Aside from the technical input, the coach must understand what it is like to play in that position. However, you can be the greatest goalkeeper in the world and yet be ineffective as a coach. This is because the whole purpose of coaching is not to demonstrate personal prowess, but to bring out the best in others.

Coaching goalkeepers is a specialist craft and many national associations, in recognising this fact, have designed goalkeeping coach education courses. I would recommend that all goalkeeping coaches seek to attain an appropriate qualification.

WHAT MAKES AN EFFECTIVE COACH?

One of the most undisputed maxims in sports coaching is: 'Fail to prepare – prepare to fail'. For all coaches, planning is a vital part of any effective coaching session. Good planning will often pre-empt problems and help the coach to achieve his objectives. In considering coaching objectives the following acronym is useful:

P urpose
A ctivity
S afety
S atisfaction

Every session should have a point to it and this objective should relate to some longer term aim. Furthermore, it is of particular value to involve the players in goal setting because, by placing them at the centre of the learning experience, it increases their motivation.

In order to provide opportunities to improve techniques and decision making, it is crucial that there is plenty of activity. However, it would be prudent to remember that it is correct practice that makes perfect. It goes without saying that the safety of the goalkeeper is of paramount importance. The coach should ensure that all factors relating to the facility, conditions, equipment and demands of the session do not put the players' safety at undue risk.

Playing soccer should be enjoyable, so sessions should be both challenging and varied. Satisfaction is further enhanced when the player believes that he is improving.

FACTORS TO CONSIDER WHEN PLANNING A SESSION

The content and delivery of the coaching programme will be determined by a number of factors, some related to the goalkeeper's personal needs and others influenced by environmental circumstances.

SIZE
When planning any session, the physical characteristics of the players must be considered. The content of the session must relate to the needs of the goalkeepers involved. For example, it would be unrealistic to cover the high cross with ten-year-olds because they are not physically capable of dealing with them and are very rarely faced with the situation during matches.

AGE

While grouping players according to age is often the most expedient method, it can be misleading since adolescents of the same age can be up to four years apart in physical development. Grouping by size, experience and ability might prove more appropriate.

EXPERIENCE

All sessions should be designed to expand on what has already been learnt. This is crucial if the keeper is to remain motivated and challenged. As with physical size, experience is a better yardstick than age.

ABILITY

The level of ability, coupled with experience, will determine how sophisticated the coaching programme will be. It is imperative that the session content challenges the players so that improvement takes place.

GROUP SIZE

In aiming for high quality goalkeeping sessions, low coach/player ratios are vital. By working with smaller groups the coach will be able to make optimum use of space and equipment and, more importantly, give each player the fullest attention.

GROUP RANGE

It is very difficult to coach a group of players where there is a wide discrepancy in size, experience and ability. If it is not possible to work with a homogeneous group, the coach should set a range of tasks suited to the individual needs of the players.

FACILITY

During winter months it is often not practicable to work in ideal conditions. Generally, at this time, the keeper has to work under floodlights on artificial surfaces. The session content should be restricted to safe practices which keep the chances of injury to a minimum (see chapter on artificial surfaces on page 107).

SAFETY

The safety of all players is of paramount importance and the coach should take appropriate steps to ensure that the facility, equipment, session structure and content do not jeopardise the keepers' health.

QUALITY OF SERVICE

In order to provide plenty of touches, many practices are conducted in pairs with the keepers serving each other. Poor feeding starves the practice, so it is vital that the goalkeepers are capable of a good standard of service.

SESSION STRUCTURE

Having reflected on the planning considerations, the coach should now prepare the session. The following structure is recommended.

Warm-up

The warm-up, which helps the body to gradually adjust from a resting state to an optimal level of readiness to train or play, has three main objectives.

- To raise the heart rate so that the base body temperature is increased.

- To warm the muscles, tendons and ligaments, and to stretch them to their working length, to reduce the chance of soft tissue injury.

- To mentally prepare the player for the task in hand and to practise some of the skills that may be required.

Warm-up exercises with the ball should always involve ball familiarity and back pass drills so that the goalkeeper becomes equally comfortable with his hands and his feet.

Explanation of session objectives

As the coaching of goalkeepers is usually conducted in small groups, sometimes even one-to-one, there is more of a dialogue between players and coach than is the case with outfield colleagues.

Therefore, it is relatively easy for the coach to tailor the session to meet individual needs. In planning training programmes, the aims should be **SMART**.

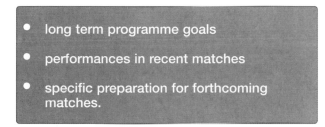

S pecific

M easurable

A greed

R ealistic

T ime related

Session objectives will be determined by a combination of:

- long term programme goals

- performances in recent matches

- specific preparation for forthcoming matches.

Prior knowledge of likely session demands and expectations will help the goalkeeper to place the practices into context and to focus on each aspect.

Technical theme

Every session should include work on polishing technique. Following the ball familiarity and ball control exercises included in the warm-up, the goalkeeper should always have the opportunity to hone his handling and footwork skills. The development of technique is dependent upon correct practice so it is imperative that the keeper receives plenty of challenging touches. The main technical theme should relate to the session objectives.

Tactical application

Good coaching is about rehearsing situations that might occur in a game, so that when they do arise the goalkeeper will be able to recognise and deal with them. It is widely acknowledged that goalkeepers are measured by the mistakes they make, so any coaching programme should be concerned with

reducing the number of errors. Since mistakes are usually due to a lapse in technique, an incorrect decision or a poor starting position, the coach should organise simulated match situations so that the keeper learns to consistently make the correct response.

Fitness

It is important that the goalkeeper is physically equipped to cope with the demands of the position. From the coach's perspective, this will entail improving:

- agility

- upper body strength

- speed

- endurance.

As players start to lose flexibility from ten years of age, it is very important to include longer stretching work to maintain suppleness. Work on flexibility is recommended when the muscles and connective tissues are warm, either in the middle or at the end of sessions.

Cool-down

A warm-down or cool-down at the end of the session is necessary for the following reasons.

- The body can gradually adjust from an active to resting state

- The body can rid itself of the waste products of exercise

- The likelihood of post exercise muscle soreness is reduced.

Debriefing

A few minutes spent summarising the key factors of a session using a question and answer technique can check the players' understanding and reinforce points for future reference.

EVALUATION

The good coach will always honestly evaluate his session to assess whether the objectives were met and to shape his planning for future sessions. The following questions may be useful.

- Did the players have fun?

- How many opportunities did they have to improve techniques and skills?

- How appropriate was the service?

- To what extent did the practices challenge them in a realistic way?

- To what extent were they able to relate the techniques and skills learnt to the game situation?

- What were the signs that the players left the session with increased confidence?

- To what extent did the session improve the players' level of understanding?

- To what degree did the session achieve the intended outcomes?

THE QUALITIES OF THE COACH

Personality

In assessing coaching effectivenss there is little doubt that the personality of the coach plays a vital role in encouraging the goalkeeper to perform to an optimal level and to play without fear. The coach's relationship with his players should reflect his overall coaching philosophy which, in turn shapes his approach to training and matches. How he broaches the task of bringing out the best in his players is just as important as what he actually does with them so it

is vital that he understands what defines him as a coach. This approach can be encapsulated in **PELE**.

Positiveness. All good coaches should seek to create a positive learning environment where players are driven by a 'can do' mentality rather than a fear of failure.

Enthusiasm. Since enjoyment is the first aim of every training session the coach must commit himself fully to ensuring that his players have fun and derive some benefit from the experience.

Leadership. As a role model the coach has to ensure that the example he sets is worthy of emulation. The coach is a very influential person, particularly in the lives of young players, and he must take this responsibility seriously.

Empowerment. Good coaching is about giving players the confidence to make decisions under pressure. To achieve this the coach must first give his players the knowledge and the opportunity to practise decision making without fear of admonishment. Players who are constantly dominated by the coach will be frightened to make their own informed decisions.

Knowledge of the subject matter

While it is not essential that the coach has been a goalkeeper, it is crucial that he has a good knowledge of the subject because the consequences of imparting incorrect information could spell disaster. The demands of the game are evolving constantly, so a coach never stops learning. The good coach has an obligation to maintain an open and enquiring mind and must move with the times.

An understanding of the player

If the coach is to apply his knowledge and experience successfully, he must understand how players learn. He must also be aware of his keeper's capabilities and how to bring out the best in him.

Observation and diagnosis of key faults

One of the coach's greatest tools is the power of observation. In order to minimise the goalkeeper's weaknesses, the coach should be able to diagnose key faults in the player's performance. These defects may be related to technical deficiencies, incorrect decisions, negative starting positions, poor physical fitness or lack of confidence.

Organisation

Having identified the fault, the coach should be able to set up a coaching situation that affords concentrated practice on a particular aspect. To do this he must be aware of the sequential nature of coaching and start at a level where the keeper can achieve success. For example, if a goalkeeper is having difficulty in dealing with high crosses during games, it would be inadvisable to begin the practice with the penalty area crowded with players. It would benefit both the player and the coach to commence with an unopposed practice where the keeper could be observed fielding crosses in isolation.

Once satisfied that the basic technique is sound and that the keeper is achieving success, by introducing defenders and then attackers, the coach can assess his player's decision making and technique under more realistic circumstances. At each stage of the progression it is essential that the keeper is regularly experiencing success before moving on to a more difficult situation. Hopefully, by the end of the session the goalkeeper will be performing effectively under simulated match conditions.

Goalkeeping coaching is not solely about exercises designed to have the keeper diving everywhere at great speed. There is a place for pressure training as part of the conditioning and fitness process, but there are very few occasions during actual matches when the keeper is faced with a barrage of shots. More importantly, the coach must remember that technique breaks down when fatigue sets in. If the practice is intended to improve technique, then the keeper should be allowed to recover between each save. Forcing the player to react in an unrealistic way might result in a rushed technique and ultimately in the development of bad habits.

Care should be taken that the quality of service is maintained through the session. The keeper should be faced with shots which he has a realistic chance of saving. He will learn very little and probably become demoralised very quickly if every shot ends up in the back of the net. Similarly, if the service is too easy and does not stretch the goalkeeper, limited progress will be made.

On a cautionary note, it should not be assumed that all finishing practice designed for strikers is valuable to goalkeepers. In the same way that playing a round of golf is not necessarily putting practice, the organisation and demands of the exercise should be tailored to the needs of the players it is supposed to benefit. Often finishing practices involve unopposed rapid-fire close range strikes giving the keeper no respite and little chance of improving his shot-stopping technique.

Communication

Throughout the coaching programme, the coach should adapt his style to suit the circumstances and to keep his players stimulated. On some occasions he may use a direct method, while on others he may use question and answer or even guide his player towards certain outcomes. Whatever style is used, the coaching points should be clear, concise, relevant and above all tailored to the level of understanding of the keeper. Where appropriate, these factors should be accompanied by a demonstration, because a visual explanation can speak a thousand words.

CONFIDENCE BUILDING

In addition to the technical aspects of coaching, one area which merits considerable attention is confidence.

WHAT IS CONFIDENCE?

Confidence is about self-belief: knowing that you will be able to handle certain situations when they arise. Above all, it is about not letting mistakes undermine faith in your own ability.

WHY IS IT IMPORTANT?

Confidence is the glue that holds the keeper's game together. It helps them to make positive decisions and to cope with pressure. Confidence also enhances consistency since it assists the goalkeeper in performing previously learnt skills and techniques.

HOW CAN THE KEEPER INCREASE HIS CONFIDENCE?

Constant polishing of strengths and improvement of weaknesses via correct practice will increase self-belief. However, the keeper must adopt a philosophical attitude to mistakes because everyone makes them. In other words, strive for perfection but do not expect it . . . at least not every time! The goalkeeper can only deal with the 'here and now' and should not dwell on mistakes because this will damage concentration.

Before matches the keeper should visualise himself playing well, and prepare physically and mentally for the game ahead. Desire is positive, fear is negative. All players should begin each game in a positive frame of mind.

HOW CAN THE COACH INCREASE THE KEEPER'S CONFIDENCE?

In training, the coach and the keeper should agree to work on areas that need attention as well as staging regular practice on the basics of head, hands, and feet. Mastery of the basic skills and techniques will give any athelete an excellent foundation on which to build his game, and goalkeepers are no different. The coach should always try to accentuate the positive and be quick to recognise progress. Coaching tricks of the trade, such as finishing every practice on a save, do wonders for self-esteem. By facing every given situation in training, the keeper will not be 'phased' when faced by similar circumstances in a game.

The coach should also work on his players' mental toughness and help them to cope with the pressures of playing in a position where one mistake can result in a goal conceded, and ultimately possible defeat. This psychological function is, without doubt, one of the most difficult aspects of goalkeeping. The coach will be the first person to whom the goalkeeper turns when things are not going well, and the coach must have the answers. When form drops confidence is affected. The coach not only has to help rectify any tactical or technical deficiencies, but also bolster self-belief. In short, the coach must not lose faith, even if the player does.

Fail to prepare and prepare to fail

One of soccer's great mysteries (and indeed one of its attractions) is that nothing is certain. There is always the chance that the unexpected might happen. This reflects the fact that all teams and their players are fallible and cannot maintain excellent form for every game. If a coach could market the unknown factor that is responsible for a great performance one weekend and a mediocre one the next, he would make a fortune. If the training is basically the same, week in week out, what is it that accounts for this inconsistency? The obvious answers are luck or the quality of the opposition, but the coach is powerless to affect either of these factors.

However, one of the aspects related to consistency that the coach or player can influence is match preparation. Match preparation entails approaching the game with the right mental attitude and in an optimum state of physical readiness. For many goalkeepers this entails following a pre-match routine that, after a time, can almost become a superstition. On occasions, the player may arrive at the ground feeling not 100% healthy or not focused, and the pre-match routine can help to dispel any listlessness and sharpen the mind and body. Having reached this desired level of readiness, it is essential that this condition is maintained throughout the match. The keeper should not lose concentration or allow himself to get cold. He should stay 'switched on' at all times.

MENTAL PREPARATION

Mental rehearsal before matches is as important as the physical warm-up. The goalkeeper should visualise previous situations in which he has played well and re-live them in his mind. By doing this he will approach the game in a positive manner. This type of mental preparation is useful in restoring confidence after a mistake in a previous game. All negative thoughts should be banished as the goalkeeper imagines himself making a string of tremendous saves.

Once into the game, no keeper will be too upset by the shot that flies into the top right-hand corner, but he will lose sleep over the one that trickles through his legs. The goalkeeper must aim to eradicate the costly mistakes from his game. If a goal is to be conceded, it should be due to brilliance on the part of the opponents, a defensive blunder in front of him, or a fluke. When this aim is realised on a regular basis, the reliability of the keeper will be confirmed and confidence will spread throughout the team.

All keepers make mistakes, but the best make the fewest. So how does he avoid letting in too many 'soft' goals? The way in which the keeper approaches a game should not alter because of the quality of the opposition. Time and time again, supposedly superior sides have come unstuck because they underestimated the other team. Thus the goalkeeper should remember to: 'Treat every shot with respect'. By religiously following this motto, concentration on the basics will be enhanced and, in turn, the number of errors will be greatly reduced.

But, despite this resolution, the odd mistake will still be made. The way in which the keeper responds after making a mistake is crucial. None of us can change history, so it is important to put mistakes at the back of your mind and get on with the rest of the match. Dwelling on mistakes during the game will affect confidence and concentration. Mistakes can be analysed afterwards and used as a learning experience. After all, we are only human and therefore prone to the odd lapse.

There are three basic types of reaction to making a mistake.

- **Confidence crumbles**. Due to one mistake, the keeper loses all faith in his ability and the positive attitude with which he began the match evaporates rapidly. Further situations, similar to the one in which the error occurred, fill him with terror. His obvious state of nervousness is recognised both by the opposition, who exploit it, and by his own team, who lose faith in him.

- **The goalkeeper tries too hard**. In an attempt to atone for his error, the keeper attempts to involve himself in situations against his better judgement. Rather than allowing play to develop and dealing with problems in the appropriate manner, he makes rash decisions in order to get to the ball quickly. He feels the need to redeem himself immediately.

- The keeper permits himself only a moment's self indulgence and gets on with the remainder of the game, **determined not to allow the error to effect his confidence or concentration**.

For the goalkeeper who provides either two of the first reactions above, one mistake can lead to another and eventually to a loss in form. The goalkeeper who can handle set backs, is the one who knows that one mistake does not make a bad player.

PHYSICAL PREPARATION

The warm-up before games may be slightly different to the one before training sessions. This is because the subsequent activity in a training session is largely controlled by the coach, allowing a gradual progression towards the targeted level of work through the use of appropriate exercises. In a game, on the other hand, the goalkeeper may be required to perform maximally in the first minute.

> The pre-match warm-up should include:
>
> - activities to raise the heart rate
>
> - stretching work
>
> - game specific movements and activities
>
> - ball work

PHASE 1

- Slow jogging – forwards, backwards and sideways.

- Preparatory stretches – calfs, hamstrings, quads, hip flexors, lower back, shoulder and upper arm – all held for no more than 6 seconds.

PHASE 2

- Faster jogging followed by striding out, slight changes of direction, high knees, heel flicks and gliding.

- Stretches as in Phase 1 but held for 10 seconds.

PHASE 3

- Striding out followed by sprinting in straight lines and zig zag patterns, then specific movements such as jumping.

- Stretches as in Phases 1 and 2 but held for 15 seconds.

- Familiarity and stretching exercises with the ball.

STATIC STRETCHES

The following stretches are recommended for each of the aforementioned phases.

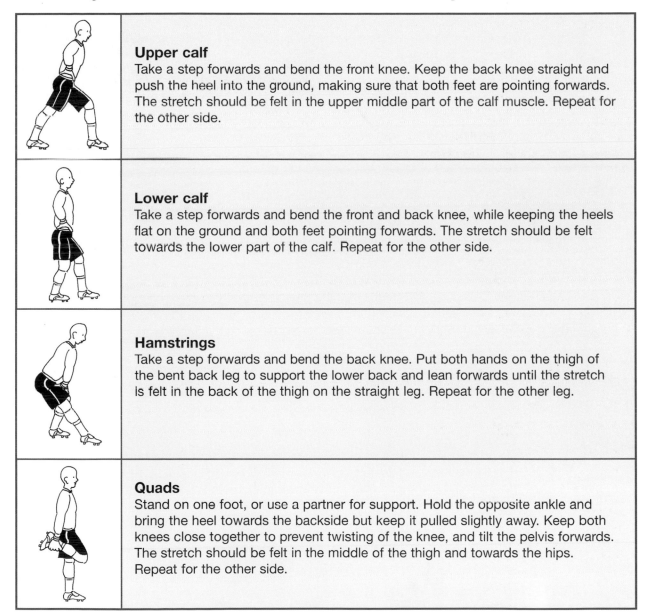

Upper calf

Take a step forwards and bend the front knee. Keep the back knee straight and push the heel into the ground, making sure that both feet are pointing forwards. The stretch should be felt in the upper middle part of the calf muscle. Repeat for the other side.

Lower calf

Take a step forwards and bend the front and back knee, while keeping the heels flat on the ground and both feet pointing forwards. The stretch should be felt towards the lower part of the calf. Repeat for the other side.

Hamstrings

Take a step forwards and bend the back knee. Put both hands on the thigh of the bent back leg to support the lower back and lean forwards until the stretch is felt in the back of the thigh on the straight leg. Repeat for the other leg.

Quads

Stand on one foot, or use a partner for support. Hold the opposite ankle and bring the heel towards the backside but keep it pulled slightly away. Keep both knees close together to prevent twisting of the knee, and tilt the pelvis forwards. The stretch should be felt in the middle of the thigh and towards the hips. Repeat for the other side.

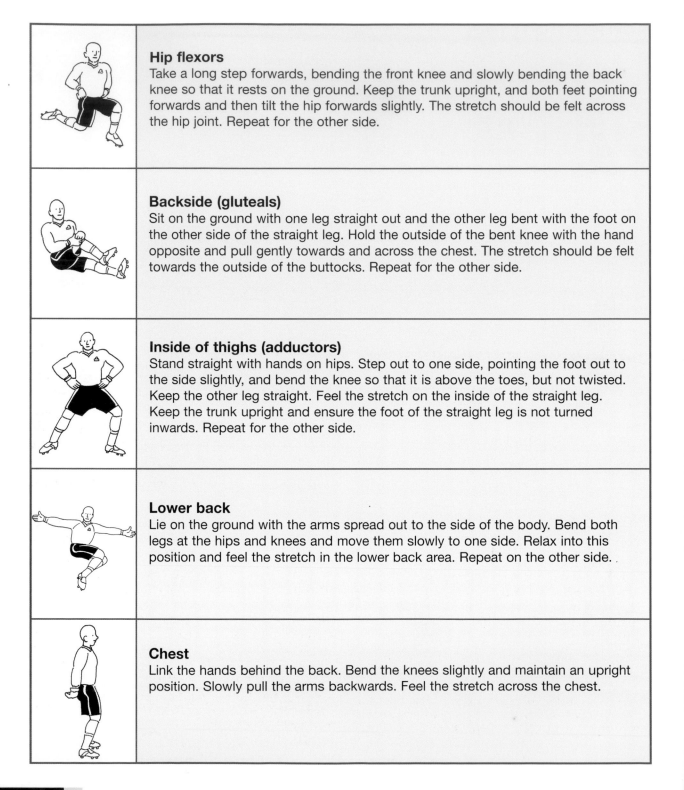

Hip flexors

Take a long step forwards, bending the front knee and slowly bending the back knee so that it rests on the ground. Keep the trunk upright, and both feet pointing forwards and then tilt the hip forwards slightly. The stretch should be felt across the hip joint. Repeat for the other side.

Backside (gluteals)

Sit on the ground with one leg straight out and the other leg bent with the foot on the other side of the straight leg. Hold the outside of the bent knee with the hand opposite and pull gently towards and across the chest. The stretch should be felt towards the outside of the buttocks. Repeat for the other side.

Inside of thighs (adductors)

Stand straight with hands on hips. Step out to one side, pointing the foot out to the side slightly, and bend the knee so that it is above the toes, but not twisted. Keep the other leg straight. Feel the stretch on the inside of the straight leg. Keep the trunk upright and ensure the foot of the straight leg is not turned inwards. Repeat for the other side.

Lower back

Lie on the ground with the arms spread out to the side of the body. Bend both legs at the hips and knees and move them slowly to one side. Relax into this position and feel the stretch in the lower back area. Repeat on the other side.

Chest

Link the hands behind the back. Bend the knees slightly and maintain an upright position. Slowly pull the arms backwards. Feel the stretch across the chest.

Shoulders
Extend the arms above the head with the hands together. Stretch the arms upwards and slightly backwards and hold at the point of slight discomfort. Slowly return to the starting point.

Shoulder and back of upper arm
Hold the elbow of the right arm with the left hand and pull the elbow behind the head until slight discomfort is felt in the back of the upper arm and the top of the shoulder. Slowly return to starting position and repeat using the left arm.

BALL FAMILIARITY EXERCISES

Select examples from Chapter 3 on ball familiarity in order to focus the mind on the task ahead.

HANDLING EXERCISES

- Comfortable body shots from 10–12 yards to warm-up the hands.

- The keeper stands on the 6-yard line and the server on the penalty spot. The server throws the ball over the head of the keeper who has to back-pedal in order to make the catch. 5 repetitions.

- Fielding crosses from both sides (throw the ball if the service is unreliable). 6 crosses from each side. Return the ball to the crosser using a variety of throws and kicks.

- Concentrated handling. The server throws or volleys the ball from a distance of 8 yards. 20 repetitions.

- From a distance of 6–8 yards the server pitches the ball in front of the keeper who has to react smartly to pick it up. 10 repetitions.

- In a 4-yard goal, the server pushes the ball from a distance of 6–8 yards to the side of the goalkeeper who dives to save. 5 repetitions on each side.

- From a distance of 12–15 yards the server drives the ball towards the keeper from the angle of the penalty area. 6 repetitions from each side of the penalty area.

- The server takes a variety of shots from the edge of the penalty area.

- The server provides ten passes that the goalkeeper has to control and return without using the hands. The service should be varied to test the keeper's control.

It is important that the goalkeeper is accompanied by another player or coach whose service is reliable so that the keeper begins the game in the best possible physical and mental state. Whether the keeper chooses to use the above exercises or not, it is vital that he acclimatises himself with the ground and weather conditions. Handling practice in the goal-mouth will give him some indication of what type of bounce to expect and what influence the sun and wind might have.

THE CARE OF EQUIPMENT

As befits his specialist position, the goalkeeper should possess a range of exclusive accessories. As part of his general preparation it is very important that he keeps his equipment in excellent working order.

BOOTS

Since one slip can result in a goal conceded, the keeper should regularly check the length of his studs to ensure that they are appropriate for the prevailing ground conditions. In simple terms, short studs for hard surfaces and long studs for muddy surfaces.

JERSEY AND SHORTS

It is essential that these two items allow for the full range of movement. A loose-fitting jersey is preferable to one that is just the right size. Shoulder and elbow padding are a matter of personal choice since it is important that the goalkeeper feels comfortable. Such padding can be useful when ground conditions are hard. The wearing of one or two undershirts is advisable on cold days. As with the jersey, shorts should be comfortable and spacious. There is a variety of styles on the market, with or without padding: once again, it is a matter of personal preference.

GOALKEEPING TROUSERS

Goalkeeping trousers are recommended for playing on icy grounds or on pitches with bare goal-mouths towards the end of the season. The bane of goalkeepers' lives is the frequent friction burns inflicted on the outside of the upper thigh by diving on hard surfaces. Such injuries could be reduced by the wearing of protective shorts or long trousers. Once again, comfort and a full range of movement should determine what is worn. If the keeper prefers not to wear trousers, then petroleum jelly smeared on the knees and thighs may reduce abrasions.

CAP

All goalkeepers should have a cap. It is a difficult skill catching in one hand while shielding the eyes from the sun with the other! The keeper should ensure that the peak is large enough and that the cap does not fall off the head too easily.

GLOVES

Although goalkeeping gloves can considerably increase the effectiveness of handling, the keeper must not forget that it is the hands inside them that are important. Even though most gloves give an excellent grip, fingers and thumbs should still be spread well to the side and behind the ball (forming a 'W' shape) if the catch is to be 100% safe.

Gloves will last longer and provide better grip if they are well maintained.

There are three steps to glove care.

- Always wash gloves immediately after matches or training in water not exceeding 86°F (30°C). A sponge will clean off surface dirt without causing abrasions to the latex palm. Do not use detergents.

- After rinsing carefully with clean water, allow the gloves to drip-dry away from direct heat or sunlight.

- Dampening the latex palm before games will improve handling. When playing in wet or muddy conditions it is recommended that the keeper takes a rag or sponge out on to the field of play so that dirt can be removed from the palm when necessary.

It is sensible to keep the newest pair of gloves for matches and to use the more worn ones for training. If conditions are particularly wet or muddy, it is advisable to use old gloves for the warm-up and to save the best pair for the match.

The ball is the enemy, but the goalkeeper should make it his friend

If players are to fulfil their potential it is essential that they are comfortable with the ball. For the goalkeeper this entails good ball control with feet as well as with the hands. As mentioned in Chapter 1, every session should incorporate practices designed to improve the goalkeeper's ability to deal with back passes. Chapter 12 will cover this at some length, but involving the keeper in outfield exercises such as 'keep ball' will do wonders for his control and passing skills.

As far as handling is concerned, the goalkeeper should be comfortable to the point of arrogance. By constantly flipping the ball back and forth using all parts of the hand and lower arm, the keeper will soon develop this 'friendship' with the ball. In the modern game, shots often swerve and dip, so the goalkeeper should be prepared to improvise and present a barrier to keep the ball out. The more familiar he is with the ball, the less likely he is to be caught off guard by a last second deviation in its flight.

This chapter will provide a number of individual exercises geared to helping the goalkeeper to be more comfortable with the ball. The list is by no means exhaustive but is as broad as the goalkeeper's or coach's imagination. It is recommended that every warm-up for either matches or training incorporates ball familiarity exercises.

BALL FAMILIARITY EXERCISES

(1) Keep the ball in the air using palms, backs of hands, wrists and forearms. Try to use a different surface on each contact. Count the number of continuous contacts before the ball hits the ground. Try to beat previous record. (See photos 1a and 1b.)

Photo 1a

Photo 1b

(2) Using the fingers of both hands, flip the ball continuously above the head. Withdraw the fingers slightly on each contact so that the ball is kept under control. (See photo 2.)

Photo 2

Photo 3

Photo 4a

Photo 4b

(3) As in (2), but this time using the fists. Progress from one hand only to both in a left-right-left-right combination. The ball should only be played 12–24 inches above head level. Again, try to beat your previous record. Having mastered this practice, try to set more difficult challenges such as going down to a kneeling and even lying position without breaking the sequence. When punching, it is important to remember the following points. (See photo 3.)

(4) Transfer the ball from one hand to the other, passing it around the body.

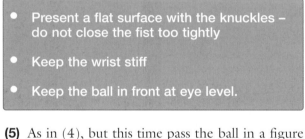

- Present a flat surface with the knuckles – do not close the fist too tightly

- Keep the wrist stiff

- Keep the ball in front at eye level.

Photo 5

Photo 6

(5) As in (4), but this time pass the ball in a figure of eight manner around and through the legs. Then try a combination of round the body and through the legs. (See photos 4a and 4b.)

(6) Hold the ball with one hand in front of the legs and the other behind. Quickly switch the position of the hands without the ball hitting the ground. (See photo 5.)

(7) Hold the ball with both hands in front of the legs. Quickly switch so that the hands move behind the legs and catch the ball before it hits the ground. (See photo 6.)

(8) Hold the ball in the right hand as high and as far away from the body as possible. In a continuous motion, sweep the ball down in front of the body, taking it in the left hand to the highest and furthest point from the body. Continue in this manner, ensuring a smooth transfer from one hand to the other.

Photo 7a

Photo 7b

Photo 8

Photo 9

down, ensure that the leading foot is placed alongside the ball and that the hands scoop up the ball in one fluid motion. (See photo 10.)

(16) Holding the ball in the hands, perform a forward roll without losing possession.

(17) Throw the ball into the air and trap it as it hits the ground. Roll out of the save so that the original standing position is regained in one smooth movement.

Photo 10

(9) Keeping both feet pointing forwards, hold the ball in the right hand, level with the shoulder. Twist the trunk so that the ball is taken to the furthest point behind the body. Repeat with the left hand. (See photos 7a and 7b.)

(10) Holding the ball out to the side of the body with the right hand, drop it and catch it again on the half-volley. Try to do this at full stretch, ensuring that the ball is caught just after it hits the ground. Repeat with the left hand. (See photo 8.)

(11) As in (10), but this time moving and picking up the ball on the half-volley.

(12) Flip the ball over the shoulder using the right hand. Back pedal quickly and arch the back to catch the ball in the left hand. (See photo 9.)

(13) Moving about the goal area, bounce the ball and catch it, checking that the fingers and thumbs form a 'W' shape. Progress to bouncing the ball like a basketball player. This is a particularly good exercise to perform before matches to enable the goalkeeper to familiarise himself with the ground conditions.

(14) Throw or kick the ball into the air and jump to catch the ball at arms length. Ensure that the ball is caught in front at eye level, with slightly bent arms and with the 'W' grip. This exercise will help the goalkeeper acclimatise to any problems caused by the sun or wind.

(15) Roll the ball along the ground and sprint to pick it up. In order to pick up without slowing

Photo 11

To execute a safe trap, the first hand goes round the ball and the second on top. (See photo 11.)

(18) Tap the ball from one foot to the other. Progress to a hop between each contact.

(19) Lightly touch the top of the ball with the sole of the foot. Alternate the feet rapidly. (See photo 12.)

(20) As in (19), but push the ball forwards for ten paces and then drag it backwards to the original starting position.

Photo 12

17

Photo 13a

Photo 13b

(21) Drop the ball to execute a wedge trap using the inside of the right foot. Repeat the movement using the outside of the right foot. Then follow the same procedure using the left foot. (See photos 13a and 13b.)

(22) Throw the ball over the head and spin around to control it using one of the techniques described in (21).

GETTING THE BASICS RIGHT – HEAD, FEET, HANDS 4

Look after the basics and the great saves will look after themselves

The majority of goalkeeping mistakes are attributable to a lapse in basic technique, so it is absolutely essential that the keeper regularly practises the fundamentals. Mastery of the basics will result in the goalkeeper making the difficult look easy and, more importantly, help to reduce the number of mistakes.

There is nothing more galling than to hear coaches or players console a keeper who has just made a glaring error by saying 'unlucky'. 'Unlucky' should refer to a deflection or some other kind of fluke and not to a lack of application of the basics. There are three fundamental areas that require constant attention.

HEAD

The head should be rock steady so that the eyes are on the ball at all times. At no point should the keeper turn his head away when making a save. It is crucial to take the ball in front of the eye-line so that it can always be seen.

FEET

Good footwork can make a difficult save look easy. Diving often involves a risk because for some time there is no barrier behind the hands. Moving quickly into line with the ball, so that some part of the body is behind the hands, will ensure that there is 'double cover'.

When preparing to receive a shot the legs should be shoulder width apart, the knees slightly bent and the weight on the balls of the feet. This is the 'ready' or 'set' position (see photo 14). If the legs

are too wide apart, it is difficult to achieve good spring and, of course, the ball might pass through them.

When scooping up a ground shot, the legs should move to less than a ball width apart. Whenever possible, body weight should be tipping forwards so that if the ball is mishandled a second save can be made almost immediately. If the ball is half-saved and the keeper falls backwards, it takes longer to recover and by that time it is usually too late.

Photo 14

HANDS

The keeper lives or dies on the strength of his handling. Good handling is the equivalent of an outfield player's 'touch', so the goalkeeper must constantly strive to perfect this all-important skill.

Frequent polishing of handling skills in training will enhance the goalkeeper's self-esteem and result in him approaching the next match in a positive frame of mind.

The majority of practices in this chapter are designed for either individual or pair work, and will prove useful in training situations where space and suitable facilities are at a premium. If the quality of practice is to be sustained, however, it is vital that the service is reliable and, with young players, the coach would be well advised to spend some time perfecting feeding techniques.

> There are four basic hand shapes when catching the ball:
>
> - The scoop – both hands behind the ball for ground shots straight at the keeper.
>
> - The cup – trapping the ball into the midriff for the waist height shots straight at the keeper.
>
> - 'W' and shock absorber – fingers and thumbs spread to the side and behind the ball (forming a 'W' shape) for shots at upper chest height and above. The forearms should be used as shock absorbers to take the pace off the ball.
>
> - Hands leading – first hand behind and second hand on top of the ball for those ground shots away from the keeper. Look for soft landings where the impact of hitting the ground is absorbed by the shoulder and side.

Photo 15   Photo 16

FOOTWORK EXERCISES

(1) RUNNING OVER BALLS/MARKERS
Organisation
Six to eight balls are laid out in a line with a ball's space in between them. The goalkeeper has to run over the balls, placing a foot in each space. (See photo 15.)

Key points
- Light, quick steps.
- Keep weight on the balls of the feet.

(2) GLIDING ROUND BALLS/MARKERS
Organisation
Six to eight balls are laid out as in (1), but this time the goalkeeper glides sideways, in and out of the balls. (See photo 16.)

Key points
- Glide with feet shoulder width apart and knees bent.
- Try to keep feet in contact with the ground as much as possible.
- Keep the body weight forward.

(3) GLIDING IN AND OUT OF BALLS/ MARKERS
Organisation
As in (2), but this time the goalkeeper approaches the balls/markers front-on. (See photo 17.)

Key points
As in (2) above.

(4) GLIDING AROUND ONE BALL
Organisation
The keeper glides around one ball in a clockwise motion. After three circuits, repeat in an anti-clockwise motion. (See photo 18.)

Key points
As in (3) above.

Photo 17

Photo 18

Photo 19

Photo 20

(5) ZIG-ZAGGING AROUND BALLS/ MARKERS

Organisation

The balls/markers are arranged in a zig-zag formation and the goalkeeper has to glide around each ball/marker. Progress to moving backwards in and out of the balls/markers. To test whether the keeper is moving with the head up, the coach can feed in the occasional ball so that the keeper has to save on the move.

Key points

- Glide with feet shoulder width apart and knees bent.

- Maintain good contact with the ground.

- Keep body weight forward.

- Try to move in the ready position with head up and hands cocked.

(6) OTHER VARIATIONS

Using his imagination the coach can devise a number of other footwork exercises that could add variety to the session. For example, side-stepping, hopping or bunny jumping over the balls. (See photos 19 and 20.)

(7) ONE-HANDED GLIDES

Organisation

Standing two paces away from the keeper, the server feeds the ball to the side, behind or in front. The keeper has to glide and catch the ball with one hand and return it to the server. As the practice develops, the server can try a few 'dummies' to check that the keeper's footwork is correct – or work with two balls to increase the intensity of the exercise.

Key points

- Glide with feet shoulder width apart, knees bent and body weight forward.

- Move on the balls of the feet.

- Try to move in line with the ball as much as possible.

- When moving backwards, use small, mincing steps.

All the aforementioned practices are not only important in their own right but are also excellent warm-up exercises.

HANDLING EXERCISES

(1) THE FOUR HAND SHAPES

Organisation

The goalkeeper kneels on the ground with the server four to six paces away. The server either throws or kicks the ball:

- along the ground straight at the keeper
- into the keeper's midriff
- towards the keeper's upper chest and head
- along the ground to the side of the keeper
- in a variety of ways to check correct decision and technique.

Key points

- For balls along the ground straight at the keeper use the scoop method with hands together behind the ball. The ball rolls into the hands and is then cradled into the body. (See photo 21.)
- For balls straight at the keeper's midriff, 'cup' the ball into the body. (See photo 22.)
- For balls towards the keeper's upper chest and head, use the shock absorber and 'W' method. Take the ball in front of the body using the forearms as shock absorbers. Fingers and thumbs spread to the side of and behind the ball to form a 'W' shape. (See photos 23a and 23b.)

Photo 23a

Photo 23b

Photo 24

- For balls on the ground away from the keeper, land on the shoulder and take the ball with the first hand behind and the second hand on top. (See photo 24.)

(2) 'Ws' AND SHOCK ABSORBER PRACTICE

Organisation

The goalkeeper sits on the ground with the server standing three to six paces away. The server volleys towards the goalkeeper's upper chest and head. (See photo 25.)

Key points

- Keep the head steady with the eyes fixed on the ball.

Photo 21

Photo 22

Photo 25

Photo 26

Photo 27

Photo 28

- Use the forearms as shock absorbers to take the pace off the ball.

- Spread fingers and thumbs to the side of and behind the ball to form a 'W' shape.

- Bring the ball back into the chest after the save.

(3) BODY SHOTS

Organisation

The ball is thrown or volleyed towards the keeper's body from a distance of 6–8 yards. Work in sets of 10/20/30. Keep a record of the number of fumbles so that the score can be beaten on the next attempt.

Key points

- Adopt the ready position with feet shoulder width apart, knees slightly bent, weight on the balls of the feet, hands ready (as if wearing handcuffs).

- For shots between waist and chest height, use the cup method.

- For shots chest height and above, use shock absorbers and 'Ws'.

- Stand firm – do not step backwards.

(4) GROUND SHOTS

Organisation

The ball is rolled towards the keeper's feet from a distance of 6–10 yards. Progress to pitching the ball at varying lengths and speeds. There are four basic methods of dealing with this type of shot and the goalkeeper must use the one he feels is most appropriate. Each of them is designed to provide a second barrier behind the hands.

Key points (long barrier method)

- Adopt the ready position.

- Bend one knee forwards and turn the other leg sideways so that a long barrier is formed.

- With both hands behind the ball, scoop it safely into the chest. (See photo 26.)

Key points (scoop method)

- Adopt the ready position.

- Move the legs to less than the width of a ball.

- With both hands behind the ball, scoop it safely into the chest. (See photo 27.)

Key points ('K' method)

- Adopt the ready position.

- Bend one knee forwards and turn the other leg sideways so that a 'K' shape is formed.

- With both hands behind the ball, scoop it safely into the chest. (See photo 28.)

Key points (the collapsing forward method recommended for those shots delivered with extra pace or slightly off-centre)

- Adopt the ready position.

- Move into the flight of the ball to scoop the ball.

Photo 29a

Photo 29b

- As the ball enters the hands, collapse the legs towards the ground.

- Cup the ball to the chest and go to ground. (See photos 29a, 29b, 29c.)

It is important that the goalkeeper masters the aforementioned techniques so that he can choose the most appropriate (and crucially the safest) method.

Photo 29c

(5) HANDLING 1 v 1
Organisation
Working in pairs using two small goals (1 yard wide) over a distance of 10–15 yards, the goalkeeper has to beat his partner with a throw. Progress to a kicked service. (See photo 30.)

Key points
- Adopt the ready position.

- Use the appropriate saving method.

(6) ONE-HANDED CATCHES
Learning to catch the ball with one hand has the benefit of teaching the goalkeeper how to take the pace off the ball (using the arms as shock absorbers). It also gives the goalkeeper tremendous confidence in his handling.

Organisation
In pairs, standing at a distance of 10–15 yards, throw the ball at varying heights and speeds to each other. Progress to standing 5 yards apart and, using two balls, throw left hand to partner's right hand while he throws left hand to your right.

Key points
- Move into line.

- Keep the head steady.

- Withdraw the arm slightly on contact to take the pace off the ball.

(7) TOP HAND SAVES
Often when saving shots bound for the top corners the keeper has to make a save with the top hand (the hand further away from the ball).

Organisation
The goalkeeper sits on the ground with the server 2 yards away. The server throws the ball to the keeper's left side and he reaches across to catch the ball using the right hand only. Repeat for the other side. (See photo 31.)

Photo 30

Photo 31

Key points

- Keep the head steady.

- Reach across the body with the top hand and catch the ball with that hand.

- Withdraw the hand slightly on impact to take the pace off the ball.

DIVING EXERCISES

For the youngster, diving is the most exciting aspect of goalkeeping. However, as in all sports, skilled performance is about making the difficult look easy and the keeper must not dive just to be spectacular. The keeper only dives when he has insufficient time to move the feet to get into line with the shot. In effect, it is an emergency action in the same way that a sliding tackle is. Many youngsters have a side on which they prefer to dive but the coach, by stripping the skill down, can diagnose the cause of this preference and rectify the weakness.

(1) FULL LENGTH DIVING
Organisation
The goalkeeper sits on his haunches. The server, standing 3 yards away, feeds the ball to the side of the keeper, who springs to catch the ball. 6 repetitions each side. Progress to crouching and then full standing position.

Key points

- Ready position (when standing).

- Lead with the hands as if wearing handcuffs.

- Push hard off near the leg.

- Shock absorber 'Ws' handling method.

- Soft landings on shoulder and side (not the elbows).

The coach should look for common faults, such as landing on the elbows or rotating, so that the body lands either flat or on the back. The cure is usually found by identifying the problem and going back to one of the more basic exercises to build up confidence.

Photo 32

(2) THE GLORY SAVE
Organisation
The goalkeeper starts in the middle of the goal. The server stands level with the post 6 yards from the line. After bouncing the ball as a signal of his intention to throw, the server feeds the ball just inside the post. The goalkeeper has to spring to save. The service increases in difficulty as the keeper progresses. (See photo 32.)

Key points

- Adopt the ready position.

- If necessary take a step (in a gliding motion).

- Good spring.

- Shock absorber 'Ws'.

- Soft landings.

(3) THE COLLAPSING SAVE
One of the most difficult saves that a keeper is faced with is the shot which passes quickly by his feet. His legs have to collapse away and he must lead with his hands because they can drop on the ball before the body can.

Organisation
The goalkeeper stands in a goal 4–5 yards in length. The server stands 6–8 yards away and passes the ball to one side of the keeper. Having made the save, the ball is returned to the server, who takes a touch before passing to the other side. The keeper must be allowed to recover and return to the ready position between saves. Progress to varied and close range service. (See photos 33a, 33b, 33c, 33d.)

Photo 33a

Photo 33b

Photo 33c

Photo 33d

Key points

- Adopt the ready position.

- React to the ball (that is, do not go down too early).

- Collapse the legs.

- Lead with both hands in front of the line of the body.

- Place the first hand behind the ball, the second hand on top of the ball.

- Soft landings (on side and shoulder).

- Pull the ball into the body.

One of the most common faults, particularly in young keepers, is the tendency to land on the elbow which causes the ball to be fumbled. By extending the arms out in front of the body, the goalkeeper will take the impact of the dive on the shoulder rather than the elbow.

SAVING ON THE MOVE EXERCISES

Since the majority of saves in matches are made while the keeper is on the move, it is essential that the coach organises exercises that develop this ability.

(1) TWO BALL
Organisation
The goalkeeper, holding a ball, faces the server who stands 2 yards away. As the server throws the ball (no.1) to the keeper's right-hand side, the keeper throws his ball (no.2) back to the server and glides to catch ball no.1. The server then throws ball no.2 to the left of the keeper, who at the same moment returns ball no.1 to the server. The process is repeated until the intended number of serves is reached. The practice requires good co-ordination between keeper and server. 20 serves will be sufficient for younger keepers. (See photo 34.)

Photo 34

Key points
- Glide into line, keeping the feet shoulder width apart.
- Keep the head steady.
- Quick hands.

(2) CATCHING AWAY FROM THE BODY
Organisation
The server stands 10–20 yards from the keeper and provides a variety of thrown and kicked services. The goalkeeper has to catch the ball without trapping it into the body. This forces him to move his feet in order to get into position to catch away from the body.

Key points
- Glide into line quickly.
- Keep the head steady.
- Choose the appropriate hand shape.

This practice is excellent for developing fast footwork combined with confident handling.

(3) MOVING INTO LINE TO SAVE
Organisation
As in (2) above, but without the restriction of catching away from the body.

Key points
As in (2) above.

(4) THE SQUARE
Organisation
The keeper works in a grid measuring 2 × 2 yards marked by discs. The coach standing two yards away serves the ball at a variety of heights. The keeper has to move quickly forwards or backwards to make the catch before the ball hits the ground.

Key points
- Quick feet.
- Keep the head steady.
- Choose the appropriate hand shape.

(5) ZIG-ZAG AND SAVE
Organisation
The keeper has to glide zig-zag fashion through a series of markers. On reaching the last marker he then has to save a shot. Progress to the server shooting at any point. (See photos 35a and 35b.)

Key points
- Glide quickly with the feet shoulder width apart.
- Lead with both hands as if wearing handcuffs.
- Keep the head steady.
- Use the appropriate handling technique.

Photo 35a

Photo 35b

(6) SAVING IN THE TRIANGLE
Organisation
The keeper stands on one side of a triangle of cones that are 6 yards apart. Two balls are placed 10–12 yards from each side with a server ready to deliver. Having dealt with the first shot, the keeper has to move rapidly to the remaining sides to make saves. He moves twice around the triangle and then rests. While this practice is performed at speed, the server should provide sufficient time for the keeper to execute proper technique. (See photo 36.)

Photo 36

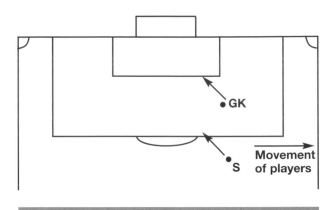

Figure 1 Saving on the move – backwards

Key points

- Move quickly between goals, trying to keep the feet shoulder width apart.

- Lead with the hands as if wearing handcuffs.

- Keep the head steady.

- Use appropriate saving technique.

(7) SAVING ON THE MOVE – FORWARDS
Organisation
There will be occasions during matches when the goalkeeper will not be properly 'set' as the shot is struck. In this exercise the keeper starts in the middle of the goal and moves quickly towards the server who then shoots.

Key points
- Keep the head steady.

- Keep calm and be prepared to improvise a save (the movement will often feel awkward as it is difficult to dive sideways while moving forwards).

(8) SAVING ON THE MOVE – BACKWARDS
Organisation
The keeper takes a position 12–18 yards from the goal line. Once the server, who is a further 10–15 yards away, plays the ball out of his feet, the keeper can move backwards into position. The server shoots for goal on his second touch. Progress from central to wide angle position. (See Figure 1.)

Key points
- Take quick, mincing steps backwards into position.

- Keep the head steady.

- Try to be in a set position, with body weight leaning forwards as the striker shoots.

- Use the appropriate saving technique.

(9) CHANGING DIRECTION TO SAVE
Organisation
The keeper glides to and fro across his goal. As he moves towards one post, the server will feed the ball in the other direction from a distance of 6–10 yards. The goalkeeper has to transfer his body weight to make the save.

Key points
- Do not anticipate the save – glide quickly.

- Glide with the feet shoulder width apart.

- When the ball is delivered, dig in and push off from the foot furthest away from the ball.

- Use the appropriate saving technique.

(10) GLIDING ACROSS THE GOAL TO SAVE

Organisation

The goalkeeper starts from the middle of the goal and glides towards the post. As he does so, the server, standing at the angle of the 6-yard box, shoots for goal. The server should vary the timing and the direction of the shot. An extra player stationed on the middle of the 6-yard line can be used to finish any knock-downs from the keeper. (See Figure 2.) The keeper must be aware that if a clean catch is not possible he cannot afford to push the ball weakly into the mid goal area as it will present any lurking forward with an easy tap-in.

Key points

- Glide quickly with the feet shoulder width apart.

- Slow down as the striker pulls back the kicking foot.

- If time allows, reduce the striker's shooting angle by getting up the line (i.e. moving towards him).

- Try to be in the set position as the shot is struck.

- Keep the head steady.

- Be prepared to save with the feet if the ball is delivered low and fast.

- If the shot cannot be gathered cleanly, it should be deflected wide of the far post or parried fiercely away from the goal.

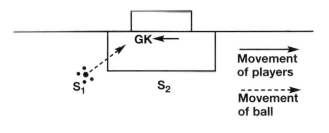

Movement of players

Movement of ball

Figure 2 Gliding across the goal to save

SHOT-STOPPING 5

Good goalkeepers make the difficult saves look easy

Having mastered the basics, the keeper should approach shot-stopping with increased confidence. The good coach will ensure that training sessions involve shots at varying heights, speeds and angles.

Throughout the practices the keeper should strive for perfection but he should realise that sometimes a save will be incomplete. On these occasions, he must react quicker than anyone else to make a second save. In short, he must not relax until the danger has been effectively nullified.

(1) 1 v 1

Organisation

Two goalkeepers face each other 15–20 yards apart, each defending a small goal (6 yards wide) using markers. The object is for each goalkeeper to score with a kick from the hands or ground.

Key points

- Get into line.
- Be 'set' as the shot is struck.
- Use the appropriate saving technique.
- React quickly to make any second saves.

(2) SHOTS IN AND AROUND THE BODY

Organisation

The server, from a distance of 15–18 yards, fires shots in and around the goalkeeper. A marker placed 1 yard inside each post is a useful guide. The server should provide a variety of volleys, half-volleys and dipping shots.

Key points

- Get into line.
- Get up the line.
- Be 'set' as the shot is struck.
- Use the appropriate saving technique.
- React quickly to make second saves.

DEFLECTING THE BALL

The keeper is not advised to use the fist to turn shots over the cross-bar or round the post. The fist is uneven and is, therefore, an unreliable means of accurately deflecting the ball to safety, whereas the fingers afford greater sensitivity and reach.

If a shot is not going to be held, the ball should be deflected for a corner or, at worst, outside the line of the posts. In the majority of cases, two hands are better than one since they present a larger barrier. However, there will be occasions when leading with one hand affords extra reach or provides the quickest reaction.

Parrying the ball straight back into play can present opponents with a secondary chance. There is a subtle difference between parrying and deflecting the ball.

Parrying the ball is recommended when the pace on the shot is so great that the keeper is not only unable to catch the ball cleanly, but also has difficulty in accurately diverting it. In this instance he should use the heels of both hands so that the ball rebounds so fiercely that it travels a good distance and is not easily controlled by the opposition. (See photo 37.)

Photo 37

Deflecting the ball is the best option for those well-directed shots which are difficult to catch. Here the goalkeeper angles the hand (or hands) and makes contact with the fingers so that the ball is diverted out of play. With practice, the keeper will learn the correct amount of resistance to be allowed by the hand. (See photo 38.) Sometimes his touch can be too strong and the ball comes back into play; on other occasions he will flick the wrist too much and merely help the ball into the net.

Photo 38

(1) CATCH OR PARRY
Organisation
This practice is designed to help the keeper to make the correct split-second decision as to whether to catch the ball or deflect it to safety. The decision is based entirely on degree of difficulty, which is determined by the placement and the pace on the shot. The server stands 10 yards from the goal and volleys the ball towards the middle of the goal with varying degrees of pace. The keeper has to decide whether to catch or parry.

Key points
- Adopt the ready position.
- 'Stay big' for as long as possible.
- Assess the pace and height of the ball.
- Decide whether to catch or parry.
- Use appropriate saving technique.
- React quickly to make any secondary saves.

(2) TURNING THE BALL OVER THE BAR
Organisation
The keeper stands on the 6-yard line with the server positioned on the penalty spot. The server feeds the ball over the keeper's head, and the keeper has to back-pedal to catch or turn the ball to safety. (See photo 39.)

Photo 39

Key points

- Adopt the ready position.

- Take small, mincing steps backwards.

- Take off on one foot.

- If the ball cannot be caught, flip it over the bar using the fingers.

(3) 2 v 2

Organisation

On a pitch measuring 20 yards in length, there are two goalkeepers in each goal. The object is to score in the opponents' goal using a throw, shot or volley. Each team may have an outfield player to capitalise on rebounds. This is a tremendously demanding and enjoyable practice in which the keepers must be competitive.

(4) QUICK-FIRE SHOTS

Organisation

This involves one goal and one keeper, with two teams of three players. The pitch is defined by the lines of the penalty area. The coach feeds in balls from the outside and players of both teams are encouraged to shoot at the earliest opportunity. (See Figure 3.)

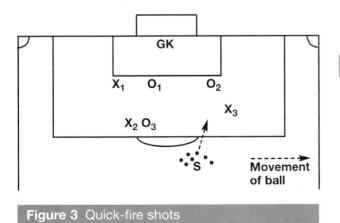

Figure 3 Quick-fire shots

(5) INSTANT SHOOTING 2 v 2

Organisation

This is a small-sided game using two goals and two keepers in an area measuring 20 x 20 yards. In this 2 v 2 situation the players are encouraged to shoot at the earliest opportunity. Spare players stand either side of each post and can be used as a 'wall' for the outfield players. The team that scores is rewarded with the next possession. (See Figure 4.)

Key points for (3), (4), (5)

- Adopt the ready position.

- Get into line quickly.

- Keep the head steady.

- Use the appropriate saving technique.

- React quickly to make any second saves.

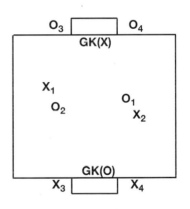

Figure 4 Instant shooting 2 v 2

Successful goalkeeping is about being in the right place at the right time

The goalkeeper who masters the art of positioning will make the job look simple. There are two basic movements involved in positioning: (1) moving into line with the ball; (2) moving up the line towards the ball. Linking these two movements is often known as 'narrowing the angle' and the purpose is to reduce the size of the target for the shooter. (See photos 40a and 40b.) The angle and distance of the ball in relation to the goal will determine the keeper's position.

The keeper basically works in an arc where the size of the angle is proportional to the distance the goalkeeper has to come down the line. (See Figure 5.) In other words, if the opponent's shooting angle is tight, there is less need to narrow the angle. The whole point of positioning is to reduce the amount of goal shown to the shooter so that if he is in a wide position his view of the goal is already diminished.

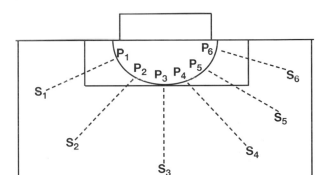

P = Position of the goalkeeper
S = Position of the server

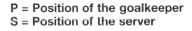

Figure 5 Positioning arc

Photo 40a

Photo 40b

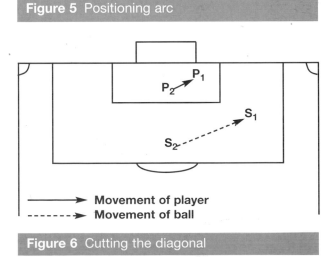

→ **Movement of player**
- - -→ **Movement of ball**

Figure 6 Cutting the diagonal

The experienced keeper will narrow the angle quickly by cutting the diagonal, gliding into line and up the line in one movement. (See Figure 6.)

The keeper should be constantly adjusting his position according to where the ball is. Even when play is in the opponents' half, he should be in line with the ball and on the edge of his penalty area, ready to make a timely interception if the ball is played over the defence.

When the ball is in and around the penalty area it is important not to come too far down the line while the ball-carrier still has his head up. The skilled player will chip a keeper who commits himself in this way. It is safer to take the final steps forwards as the ball-carrier is preparing to shoot and has his eyes fixed on the ball.

Finally, it is imperative that the keeper is 'set' in the ready position as the shot is struck, because it is difficult to dive sideways while still moving forwards.

(1) HANDBALL

Organisation

The goalkeeper takes up a position in the middle of the goal. Four servers are stationed around the penalty area. They throw the ball to each other and the keeper has to take up an appropriate position. After each catch, the server should pause so that the coach can assess the keeper's position. Progress to the servers occasionally volleying the ball towards the goal. (See Figure 7.)

Key points

- Always expect a shot.

- Get into line – where possible glide in the ready position.

- Get up the line – where possible glide in the ready position.

- Be 'set' in the ready position as the shot is struck.

- Use the appropriate saving technique.

- React quickly to make any second saves.

(2) ANGLED SHOTS

Organisation

The coach cones off the goal-mouth in sectors (see Figure 8) which are then numbered one to five. A server with a ball is stationed in each sector. On the coach's command one of the servers plays the ball out of his feet and shoots for goal. The goalkeeper reacts to the command by getting into position as quickly as possible.

Key points

- Always expect a shot.

- Cut the diagonal (into line and up the line).

- Glide in the ready position.

- Be 'set' in the ready position as the ball is struck.

- Use the appropriate saving technique.

- React quickly to make any second saves.

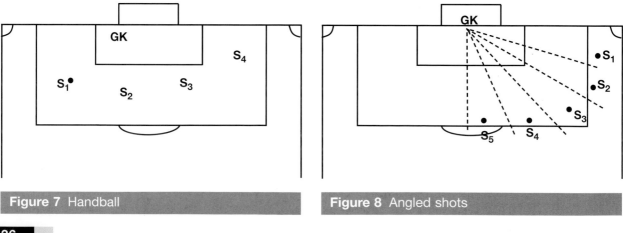

Figure 7 Handball

Figure 8 Angled shots

(3) OFF THE CONES AND SHOOT

Organisation

Three heavy-weight cones are bunched together on the edge of the penalty area. The server throws the ball at the cones and fires in the rebound. The keeper makes the save. Occasionally the ball may squeeze through the cones and the keeper must be ready to advance quickly to gather it. Using the cones as a rebounding surface leads to unpredictable shooting angles and therefore keeps the goalkeeper on his toes.

Key points

- Adopt a good starting position.

- Expect a shot at any time.

- Cut the diagonal (into line and up the line).

- Steal an extra step forwards as the shooter addresses the ball.

- Be 'set' in the ready position as the ball is struck.

- Use the appropriate saving technique.

- React quickly to make any second saves.

(4) TURN AND SAVE

Organisation

For this practice the server changes position after every shot and always shoots on the move. The keeper faces the goal and turns on the command. The server waits for the keeper to pick up the line of the ball before shooting.

Key points

- Adopt a good starting position relative to the ball, usually 3–4 yards off the goal line.

- Pick up the line of the ball quickly.

- Cut the diagonal.

- Be 'set' in the ready position as the ball is struck.

- Use the appropriate saving technique.

- React quickly to make any second saves.

(5) PASS AND SHOOT

Organisation

In this practice four servers stand in a fan formation 15–18 yards from the goal either in central or wide positions. One of the servers on the outside passes the ball into the central player who either lays it off to one of his colleagues or turns to shoot himself. The keeper has to respond in the appropriate manner. (See Figure 9.)

Key points

As in (4) above.

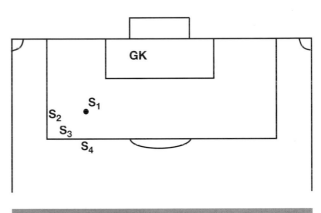

Figure 9 Pass and shoot

(6) SHOOTING GALLERY

Organisation

The coach stands behind the goalkeeper who is faced by a number of servers spread around the edge of the penalty, each with a ball. The coach points to one server who plays the ball out of his feet and shoots for goal. The keeper has to react quickly to get into line. (See Figure 10.)

Key points

- Pick up the line of the ball quickly.

- Cut the diagonal (into line and up the line).

- Steal an extra step forwards as the shooter addresses the ball.

- Be 'set' in the ready position as the ball is struck.

- Use the appropriate saving technique.

- React quickly to make any second saves.

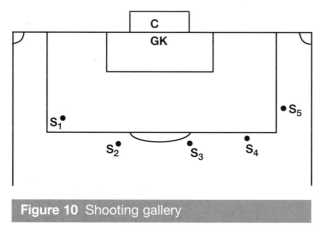

Figure 10 Shooting gallery

(7) 4 v 2

Organisation

The coach marks out a corridor in an arc shape between the penalty spot and the edge of the 'D'. (See Figure 11.) Four attackers play against two defenders in the corridor. The ball is fed to the strikers by one of two servers positioned outside the shooting corridor. The idea is for the attackers to score as many goals as possible from shots inside the corridor. Players are only allowed out of the corridor to react to rebounds from the goalkeeper. Having made the save the keeper throws the ball to one of the servers.

Key points

- Always expect a shot.

- Adopt a good starting position.

- Cut the diagonal (into line and up the line).

- Steal an extra step forwards as the shooter addresses the ball.

- Be 'set' in the ready position as the ball is struck.

- Use the appropriate saving technique.

- React quickly to make any second saves.

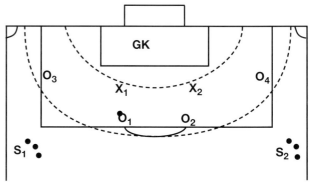

Figure 11 4 v 2

Always be prepared for the unexpected

The work that a goalkeeper has to cope with is not always straightforward because there is a constantly changing scene in front of him. Team mates as well as opponents make life difficult by blocking his field of vision. There are times when the ball is seen very late, when deflections or cut-backs momentarily catch the keeper out of position and when opponents use trickery to chip and swerve shots. Often the situation will necessitate some last-minute improvisation on his part. For example, he might use a trailing leg to clear the ball after being wrong-footed by a deflection.

Some people might argue that you cannot coach players to deal with the unexpected because they will act instinctively anyway. However, if in training the coach can re-create these unpredictable situations, the goalkeeper will know how to react when it happens again and, who knows, it might be the save that turns the game.

(1) FORWARD ROLL AND SAVE
Organisation
The goalkeeper stands in the middle of his goal and completes a forward roll. As he is getting to his feet the server shoots from 12–15 yards. The keeper makes the save.

Key points
- Take the weight on the shoulders.
- Try to come out of the roll in the ready position.
- Keep the head steady.
- Use the appropriate saving technique (but be prepared to improvise using any body part as a barrier).

- React quickly to make any second save

(2) SAVING FROM A SITTING POSITION
Organisation
The keeper sits and on the command 'Up!' gets to his feet. As the keeper rises the server shoots from a distance of 6–10 yards. (See photo 41.)

Key points
- Get up as quickly as possible.
- Keep the head steady.
- Use the appropriate saving technique.
- React quickly to make any second saves.

Photo 41

(3) SAVING THE CHIP
Organisation
The goalkeeper sits on his 6-yard line (further out for more experienced players) and the server stands just outside the penalty area. At the first signs of movement from the keeper, the server chips the ball towards the goal. The keeper has to make the save. Sharpen the keeper's competitive edge by recording the score out of ten.

Key points

- Get up quickly.

- Keep the head steady.

- Take rapid, mincing steps backwards before attempting to save.

- Catch or deflect to safety.

(4) THE CUT-BACK

Organisation

The server starts with the ball on the angle of the penalty area and the keeper reacts to this position. The server moves across the area to a marker, at which he attempts to cut the ball back inside the near post. The practice is repeated from the other side of the area. As the keeper becomes more proficient the server can vary the timing and angle of the shot. (See Figure 12.)

Key points

- Get into line with the ball.

- Glide with the feet shoulder width apart.

- Do not be pulled too far across the goal.

- Get up line if possible.

- Be 'set' in the ready position as the shot is struck.

- Use the appropriate saving method.

- React quickly to make any second save.

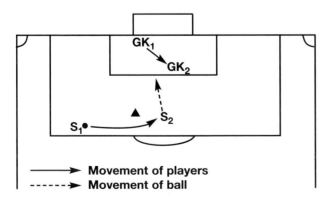

Figure 12 The cut-back

(5) NO-HOPE ALLEY

Organisation

The keeper stands at one post facing out towards the touch-line. The server, standing 15–20 yards from the goal line, shouts 'Turn!'. Once the keeper has spun round and is starting to cross the goal-mouth, the server shoots for the empty corner. Repeat the practice from the other side of the goal. (See Figure 13.)

Key points

- Look to get into line as quickly as possible.

- If there's time, get up the line.

- Glide rather than run.

- Keep the head steady.

- Use the appropriate saving method.

- React quickly to make any second saves.

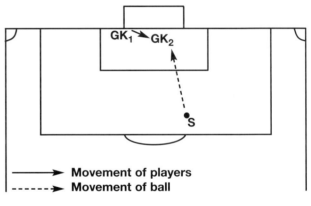

Figure 13 No-hope alley

(6) EVEN-LESS-HOPE ALLEY

Organisation

The goalkeeper takes up a position in the goal-mouth as if having made a sprawling save – lying, sitting or kneeling. As the server, who is positioned just outside the penalty area, plays the ball out of his feet and is preparing to shoot, the goalkeeper is allowed to rise to his feet and get into position. The keeper should vary his position each time. (See photos 42a, 42b, 42c and 42d.)

Photo 42a

Photo 42b

Photo 42c

Photo 42d

Key points

- Get to your feet as quickly as possible.

- Move into line quickly.

- Glide rather than run.

- Keep the head steady.

- Use the appropriate saving technique.

- React quickly to make any second saves.

(7) DEFLECTIONS USING CONES

Organisation

Four or five large, heavy cones are placed 8 yards from the goal line. The server shoots from 18–20 yards, aiming to deflect the ball off the cones. The keeper has to save.

Key points

- Adopt the ready position.

- Do not get too close to the cones (because it affords less reaction time).

- Keep the head steady.

- Do not panic if the ball is momentarily unsighted or deflected.

- Go for the first shot but be prepared to improvise if the ball is deflected.

(8) DEFLECTIONS USING OTHER PLAYERS

Organisation

This practice is very similar to (8), but this time the cones are replaced by one or two outfield players who can make life difficult by obscuring the keeper's view and deflecting or dummying the ball. These players will capitalise on any loose handling. (See photo 43.)

Key points

- Adopt the ready position.

- Do not be distracted by the player(s) in front.

Photo 43

- Get a view of the ball without compromising the starting position or becoming unbalanced.

- Do not get too close to the player(s) in front.

- Keep the head steady.

- Go for the first shot but be ready to improvise if the ball is deflected.

- React quickly to make any second save.

(9) SAVING WITH THE FEET

Saving with the feet has become accepted practice in certain situations. If the pace and close proximity of the shot make safe handling impossible, the feet and the legs are the next best barrier. Little back-lift is required because the goalkeeper can easily use the pace on the ball to re-direct it to safety.

Organisation

The goalkeeper defends a small goal 1 yard wide. The server shoots low and hard from a distance of 5 yards. The keeper is not allowed to save with the hands and must use the feet or legs. Progress to varying the service and allow the keeper to use the hands when appropriate. (See photo 44.)

Key points

- Keep the head steady.

- Keep the legs less than a ball width apart.

- Turn the feet outwards to present a large barrier.

- Use little back-lift.

- Re-direct the ball to safety.

Photo 44

(10) SAVING WITH THE FEET OR HANDS BARRAGE

Organisation

The keeper stands on his goal line faced by ten balls placed along the 6-yard box. There is a server at each end. The server at one end fires a shot straight at the keeper. As soon as he has saved, a shot arrives from the second server. The servers should vary the height of the shots. This process continues until all of the balls have been kicked. The service must be rapid but controlled. (See photo 45.)

Key points

- Keep the head steady.

- Adopt the ready position.

- Make the correct decision (to save with the feet or hands).

- Use the correct saving technique.

Photo 45

(11) SECOND SAVES

There will be occasions when shots cannot be dealt with cleanly and the goalkeeper must have a good attitude towards second saves. This requires him to rise quickly to provide the best possible chance of dealing with any follow-up shots. Second saves are much easier to perform when the keeper's body weight has been falling forwards in the initial stop.

Organisation

The keeper lies on his front with his head 4 yards from the post. The server stands 4–6 yards away. On the server's command the keeper rises and the ball is played inside the post. The keeper has to react to prevent the ball from crossing the line. Progress to starting in different positions such as lying on the side and back.

Key points

- Rise quickly to provide a platform from which to dive (i.e. wholly or partly on the feet).

- Keep the head steady.

- If necessary, improvise to keep the ball out.

- Do not relax until the ball is safe.

(12) WRESTLING TO SAVE

Organisation

The goalkeeper stands in the middle of the goal ready to face a shot from the server standing at the edge of the penalty area. Before the shot is delivered, the keeper is manhandled by another player (preferably of a similar physique) and he has to break free before making the save. The practice is demanding and should be repeated between six to ten times, depending on the level of the performer.

Key points

- Get into position as soon as possible.

- Be prepared to improvise a save if off balance.

- React quickly to make any second save.

(13) LONG RANGE SHOTS

Ironically, long shots can present more of a problem than short range ones due to the fact that there is more time for the ball to move in flight. The goalkeeper should follow the basic rules of getting in line but must not panic if the ball dips or swerves at the last second. The save might look ungainly but artistic merit is not an objective!

Organisation

The server occupies a position just outside of the penalty area. Using volleys, half-volleys and ground shots, he provides the keeper with a varied bombardment.

Key points

- Get into line and up the line.

- Get 'set' in the ready position as the shot is struck.

- Keep the head steady.

- Apply the appropriate saving technique.

- If the ball deviates, stay calm and improvise if necessary.

- React quickly to make any second save.

(14) LONG RANGE SHOTS SMALL-SIDED GAME

Organisation

This practice takes place in an area 40 x 40 yards. Each team has three defenders and two attackers. Defenders must remain in their own half and attackers in their opponents' half. The aim is for the defenders to create shooting opportunities for themselves. The attackers try to make it difficult for the opposition by dummying and deflecting shots. (See Figure 14.)

Key points

As in (13 above).

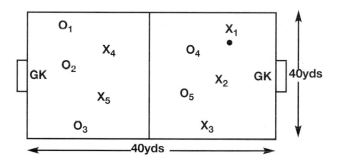

Figure 14 Long range shots small-sided game

REACTION SAVES 8

Quick reactions are vital to successful goalkeeping

There is a commonly held belief that instinctive elements of skilled performance, such as reaction saves, cannot be coached. This is not entirely true as reaction time can be improved through practice. By rehearsing game-like scenarios in training, the goalkeeper can be more effective in dealing with close range shots and headers. Commentators often refer to 'reflex saves' to describe those occasions when the keeper reacts extremely quickly to deal with what appears to be a certain goal.

Reaction saves are usually a combination of good technique and improvisation. The technical element will probably involve quick footwork to arrive at the right place at the right time. An improvised save is likely to be required when there is insufficient time to deal with the shot or header in a more conventional manner.

The most common failing of goalkeepers when faced with a close range shot is the tendency to go to ground too early. He must stay on his feet to provide the biggest barrier and reach as possible. Secondly he must keep his head still with eyes focussed on the ball. This is not easy for young goalkeepers to achieve as the natural inclination is to seek evasive action when a player is about to blast the ball goalwards from short range! By 'staying big' the keeper will not only fill up the goal but also be in a better position to readjust if the initial effort is blocked.

As the speed of the shot or header might not allow the application of conventional saving technique, the keeper must be prepared to improvise and use any body part to keep the ball out of the net. In this case the end does justify the means and the fact that the save may be made with a foot, knee or shoulder is immaterial. As in all cases of course, the keeper should be ready to make a second save if required.

In the split second that the keeper has to react he has to assess whether he is going to block the ball or save it. There is a subtle difference between blocking and saving. Blocking is used when the keeper decides to use his body as a barrier and hopes that the shot hits him and rebounds to safety. Saving involves a deliberate act of using the hands or feet to deal with the shot and is employed when the keeper has more time to see the ball. In some instances the experienced keeper will actually step backwards to buy himself more time. In contrast blocking is used as a last resort (see Chapter 9).

(1) SPIN AND DROP
Organisation
The keeper stands with his legs open, facing the server standing 2–3 yards away. The server passes the ball through the keeper's legs and he has to spin and dive to save. The exercise is repeated ten times with the keeper alternating the direction in which he spins.

Key points
- Spin quickly keeping the head steady.

- Dive with the first hand reaching round the far side of the ball and the second hand on top.

- Pull the ball into the body for safety.

(2) THROUGH THE LEGS AND DROP

Organisation

The keeper stands with his legs open, facing away from the server who stands 2–3 yards away. The server passes the ball through the goalkeeper's legs who dives to save. The exercise is repeated ten times.

Key points

- Dive with the first hand reaching round the far side of the ball and the second hand on top.

- Be prepared to move the feet if the ball is delivered quickly.

- Pull the ball into the body for safety.

(3) ONE TOUCH RETURNS

Organisation

The goalkeeper stands in the goal 6 yards wide with a supply of balls behind him. The keeper rolls the ball out to the server standing 4–6 yards away. The server returns a first time shot at varying heights.

Key points

- React to the shot, do not go to ground too early.

- Keep the head steady.

- Use the appropriate hand shape to gather the ball.

- Be ready to make a second save if required.

(4) THROUGH THE LEGS, SPIN AND SAVE

Organisation

The goalkeeper stands in a goal 4 yards wide with his back to the server. He feeds the ball through his legs, spins and prepares to receive a shot from the server standing at varying distances. The keeper alternates the direction in which he spins.

Key points

- Spin quickly with the head steady.

- React to the shot, do not go to ground too early.

- Be prepared to improvise if there is insufficient time to gather the ball cleanly.

- Be ready to make a second save if required.

(5) SPIN AND SAVE

Organisation

The goalkeeper faces the goal. On the command 'Turn!' from the server, who stands at varying distances, he turns to save the shot. The exercise is repeated in sets of ten.

Key points

- Spin quickly with the head steady.

- Get into line and up the line if time allows.

- Be prepared to improvise if there is insufficient time to gather the ball cleanly.

- Be ready to make a second save if required.

(6) THE PULL BACK

Organisation

The goalkeeper faces Server 1 standing outside the line of the post. He plays a crisp pass to Server 2 positioned 6–8 yards from goal. Server 2 moving into the flight of the pass shoots into the near part of the goal. The keeper has to move quickly to face the striker and make the save (see Figure 15). The exercise is repeated in sets of ten.

Key points

- Turn and move across the goal quickly with the head steady.

- Choose the appropriate saving technique but be prepared to improvise if necessary.

- Be ready to make a second save if required.

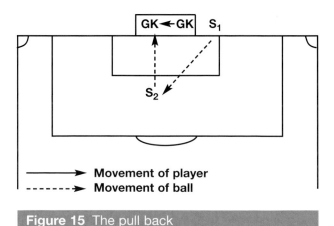

Figure 15 The pull back

(7) CLOSE RANGE VOLLEYS

Organisation

The goalkeeper faces Server 1 standing outside the line of the post. He feeds by hand to Server 2 positioned 4–6 yards from goal. Server 2 side foot volleys the ball towards the near part of the goal. The keeper has to move quickly to face the striker and make the save (see Figure 16). The exercise is repeated in sets of ten.

Key points

- Turn quickly with the head steady.

- Stay big and stay deep to increase reaction time.

- Be prepared to improvise if there is insufficient time to gather the ball cleanly.

- Be ready to make a second save if required.

(8) CLOSE RANGE HEADERS

Organisation

Server 1 stands behind the goalkeeper who faces Server 2. Server 1 hand feeds the ball to Server 2 who heads for goal from 4–6 yards.

Key points

- Stay big and stay deep.

- Be prepared to improvise if there is insufficient time to gather the ball cleanly.

- Be ready to make a second save if required.

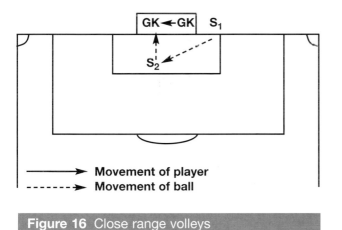

Figure 16 Close range volleys

ONE-AGAINST-ONE SITUATIONS 9

With the exception of saving a penalty, the closest a goalkeeper can get to scoring a goal is to save in a one-against-one situation

By preventing the player from scoring a certain goal, the keeper can lift his team-mates and demoralise the opposition. Saving in one-against-one situations more often than not requires good judgement combined with raw courage. However, if the technique is executed properly and with conviction, injury to the goalkeeper seldom results. Everyone expects a goal to be scored when a player is clear of the defence – that is, everyone except the keeper! It is essential that he is mentally aggressive and is determined not to be beaten. If a goal is going to be conceded, he must make the opponent earn his reward.

> There are three stages in saving in one-against-one situations.
>
> - Assessment of the situation.
>
> - Decision.
>
> - Application of the appropriate technique.

When the ball is played in behind the defence or when the attacker breaks through, the goalkeeper must resist the temptation to react instinctively and instead rapidly weigh up the situation. His judgement must be based on the resolution to make life as difficult as possible for the ball carrier. Basically, he has to choose whether to rush the opponent or to hold his ground.

In all one-against-one situations the goalkeeper must take great care not to foul the opponent because the double punishment of a penalty kick conceded and dismissal from the field usually follows. For this reason, the keeper's reading of the situation, his decision, and his saving technique must be perfect.

If the opponent has good control of the ball, it is not advisable for the keeper to rush him. By committing himself when there is little chance of winning possession or blocking the shot, the keeper will only succeed in making life easier for the ball carrier. Once the keeper goes to ground he is momentarily out of the game so he must stay on his feet unless he is sure of winning the ball.

As the player approaches he is under pressure because a goal is expected, and he is further stressed by the numerous alternatives open to him. Does he take the ball round the keeper, attempt a chip, a side-foot shot or a blast? The keeper who rushes impetuously in this situation makes up the mind of the ball carrier, who will neatly side-step the rash lunge and put the ball into the net.

If the player has close control of the ball, the keeper must stay on his feet in an attempt to 'buy' himself time and, better still, to force his opponent wide so that the shooting angle is reduced. Recovering defenders should be encouraged to get across the path of the ball carrier in order to reduce his options.

The following scenarios may help to clarify the most appropriate course of action.

Scenario 1: the ball is played into space behind the defence

Assessment
The keeper judges the relative distances that he and the nearest opponent are to the ball.

Decision
Based on the assessment that at best he is going to get to the ball first or at worst at the same time as the opponent, the keeper decides to attack and moves quickly without hesitation. In the last few paces he realises that he will need to dive to win possession.

Technique
To win possession the goalkeeper dives into the path of the ball and, with one hand behind and one on top, traps it. As the ball is collected it is quickly brought into the chest. He provides further protection by tucking in the head and legs. To block the ball the keeper leads with the hands to present the widest barrier possible. To counteract skilful opponents who will try to lift the ball over the diving body, the keeper can raise the top arm. Leading with the feet is not recommended as this reduces the size of the barrier.

Scenario 2: the opponent dribbles through the defence

Assessment
The keeper evaluates the ball carrier's control.

Decision (a)
The keeper recognises that the opponent's last touch is heavy and he has momentarily lost control. The keeper decides to advance to either win the ball outright or to execute a block.

Technique (a)
The keeper responds as in scenario 1.

Decision (b)
The keeper realises that the ball carrier has good control and decides to buy time for fellow defenders to recover and to put pressure on the opponent.

Technique (b)
The keeper advances slowly and narrows the angle trying to force the opponent wide. He stays on his feet and prepares to save the shot. The opponent is likely to shoot hard and low close to the keeper, so it is recommended that he keeps a low ready position and is prepared to save with the feet.

Scenario 3: the ball breaks to an unmarked opponent very close to the goal

Assessment
The keeper judges the degree of immediate danger.

Decision
As there is very little time, the keeper decides to rush the opponent in order to block the shot.

Technique
The keeper advances rapidly and spreads his body to present the largest possible barrier. The ploy is to panic the opponent into shooting quickly and inaccurately.

(1) DIVING AT FEET FROM A KNEELING, CROUCHING AND STANDING POSITION

Organisation

These progressive practices are designed to introduce young players to diving at feet in a way that induces confidence. As the keeper kneels, the server walks past with the ball at his feet. Progress to the keeper crouching and then standing with the server running with the ball. (See photo 46.)

Key points

- Time the dive correctly – take the ball, not the player.

- Lead with the hands.

- Keep the head steady and the eyes open.

- Claim the ball with one hand behind and one on top.

- Pull the ball into the chest.

- Tuck in the head and legs for additional protection.

Photo 46

(2) HEAD-FIRST DIVING AT FEET

Organisation

As in practice (1) but this time the server approaches the goalkeeper head-on. (See photo 47.)

Key points

- Time the dive correctly – take the ball, not the player.

- Lead with the hands.

- Keep the head steady and the eyes open.

- First hand reaches round the front of the ball, second hand on top of the ball.

- Pull the ball into the chest.

- Tuck in the head and legs for additional protection.

Photo 47

(3) 2 v 1 SAVING AT FEET

Organisation

Two players and one goalkeeper play in a grid measuring 10 yards x 10 yards. The players attempt to keep possession while the keeper aims either to claim the ball or to divert it out of the grid. The keeper is allowed to attack the ball after the first pass. After gaining five successes the goalkeeper rests. (See Figure 17.)

Key points

- Adopt a low ready position with the hands by the side of the feet.

- Stay on the feet unless you are sure of winning the ball.

- Assess the situation, looking for any mis-control.

- Threaten the ball carrier by feinting.

- Try to manoeuvre the ball carrier into a tight space (for example, a corner or a line).

- When diving, lead with the hands presenting a long barrier.

- Be committed with the head steady and the eyes open.

- Do not foul.

(4) 1 v 1 DRIBBLING AROUND THE GOALKEEPER

Organisation

In a grid measuring 10 yards x 10 yards the server has to round the keeper to score into a goal 3 yards wide. (See photo 48.)

Key points

- Adopt a low ready position with the hands by the side of the feet.

- Stay on the feet unless you are sure of winning the ball.

- Try to force the ball carrier away from the goal.

- Look to attack if the player miscontrols the ball.

- When diving, lead with the hands presenting a long barrier.

- Be committed with the head steady and the eyes open.

- Do not foul.

Photo 48

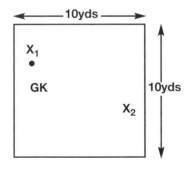

Figure 17 2 v 1 saving at feet

(5) 1 v 1 SCORING PAST THE GOALKEEPER

Organisation

In a grid measuring 10 yards x 10 yards the keeper throws a fast ball to the server who controls to score into a goal 3 yards wide. The server can score with a shot or by dribbling around the keeper. If the server's first touch is poor, the keeper will have the opportunity to attack. On the other hand if his control is good, then staying on the feet is recommended. The server should vary his starting position to test the goalkeeper's understanding of how to force the ball carrier wide.

Key points

- Assess the server's first touch.

- If attacking, lead with the hands presenting a large barrier.

- Stay on the feet unless you are sure of winning the ball.

- Put pressure on the server.

- Try to force the server wide.

- Be prepared to save with the feet if necessary.

- Do not foul.

(6) BLOCKING

Organisation

Six balls are placed in an arc 10 yards from the goal. As the server moves towards the ball, the keeper has to advance to block the shot. The goalkeeper then returns to his starting position and the exercise is repeated. (See Figure 18.)

Key points

- Cover the ground quickly.

- Stay big and use the body as a barrier.

- Keep the eyes open.

- Be prepared to make a second save if necessary.

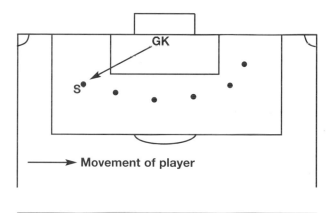

Figure 18 Blocking

(7) SPREADING

Organisation

Server 1 is positioned 3 yards wide of the six yard line while server 2 stands between 6–8 yards from the goal line. Server 1 plays to Server 2 who is conditioned to shoot on his second touch. Server 2 has a heavy first touch so that the goalkeeper is able to attack the ball with his hands.

Key points

- Close down the shooter quickly as the ball is travelling and assess whether to win the ball outright or block it.

- If winning the ball lead with both hands.

- If the shooter gets to the ball first spread the hands to provide the biggest possible barrier (see photo 49).

- Be committed and keep the eyes open.

- Get up quickly to make a second save if required.

Photo 49

(8) PLUNGING

Organisation

The server stands six yards from the goal line with a player on either side. The goalkeeper stands on the line facing the server who feeds the ball between the keeper and one of the players (see Figure 19). The service should be rolled or bounced so that the keeper has to deal with balls at varying heights. Depending on his proximity to the ball the keeper has to decide to claim it outright or to execute a block.

Key points

- Decide whether to win the ball or block,

- Be committed and keep the eyes open whatever the course of action.

- If attempting to win the ball lead with the hands.

- If blocking stay big and use the body as a barrier.

- Be prepared to make a second save if neccssary.

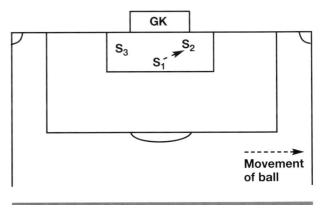

Figure 19 Plunging

(9) THE THROUGH BALL

Organisation

From a distance of 35 yards from goal, the coach plays the ball in front of an attacking player (standing 30 yards from goal) who has to control to score. The coach can vary the pace and angle of the pass to test the keeper's judgement of when to attack the ball and when to hold his ground. (See Figure 20.)

Key points

- Adopt a good position (advanced enough to intercept an overhit ball, but not too far off the line to be vulnerable to the chip).

- Assess the situation.

- Make the correct decision.

- Apply the appropriate technique.

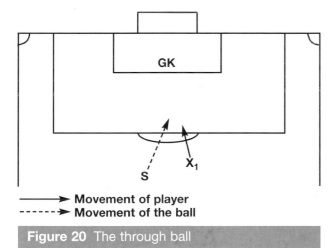

⟶ **Movement of player**
----⟶ **Movement of the ball**

Figure 20 The through ball

(10) THE SHOOT-OUT

Organisation

The ball carrier sets off 35 yards from goal with a defender in pursuit starting 5 yards behind him. The goalkeeper and defender have to deal with the situation. The coach can vary the starting position of the attackers and defenders to re-create game situations. (See Figure 21.)

Key points

- Adopt a good starting position (advanced enough to intercept an overhit ball, but not too far off the line to be vulnerable to the chip).

- Come down the line cautiously to narrow the angle.

- Assess the ball carrier's control and the position of the defender.

- If the ball carrier has good ball control, stay on the feet to 'buy' time.

- Put pressure on the player by threatening the ball.

- Try to force the opponent wide.

- If attempting to win the ball lead with the hands.

- If blocking stay big and use the body as a barrier.

- Be prepared to save with the feet if necessary.

- Maintain good communication with the recovering defender.

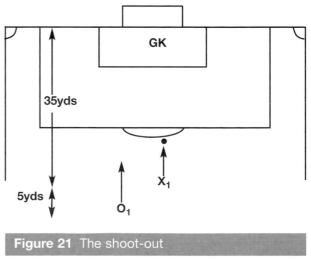

Figure 21 The shoot-out

(11) SMALL-SIDED GAME – BREAK OUT
Organisation
The practice takes the form of a small-sided game (four against four including two goalkeepers) in an area measuring 60 yards x 40 yards. For the purpose of the practice the pitch is divided into three equal sections and outfield players are restricted to the middle third of the pitch unless the ball is either played into one of the end zones or a player dribbles through into one of the end zones. Only one player from each team is allowed to enter the end zone. The aim of the practice is to give the keeper experience of realistic one-against-one situations. (See Figure 22.)

Key points
- Adopt a good starting position but always expect a shot.

- Be ready to intercept through-balls.

- Assess the situation.

- Make the correct decision.

- If the ball carrier has control, 'buy' time and force him wide.

- When diving at feet, make a long barrier with the body. Raise the top arm if necessary.

- When blocking stay big and use the body as a barrier.

- Do not foul.

- Be prepared to save close shots with the feet.

- Maintain good communication with the recovering defender.

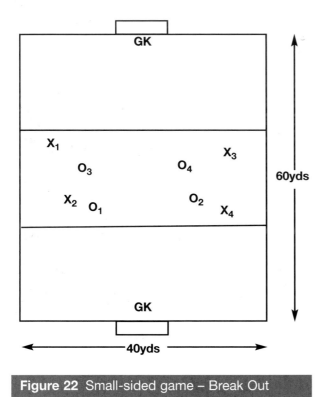

Figure 22 Small-sided game – Break Out

Dealing with the high cross is the yardstick by which top goalkeepers are measured

This is without doubt the most difficult aspect of goalkeeping, since it requires crucial decision-making combined with the application of good technique under pressure. As a large percentage of goals result from high balls played into the penalty area, a keeper's worth is often measured in terms of his ability to deal effectively with crosses.

Goalkeepers who consistently come to gather crosses are always very popular with their teammates because it makes their job much easier. However, while no-one would appreciate a goalkeeper who never leaves his line, the keeper who has a cavalier approach and goes for every cross can also become a liability.

The goalkeeper must work with his fellow defenders to deal effectively with the ball played into the box. Myths such as 'Every cross into the 6-yard box must be the goalkeeper's' raise unrealistic expectations. Sometimes, such as on near post corners or low-driven crosses, defenders may be better placed to deal with the problem.

Nevertheless, the keeper must realise that he has a responsibility to use the advantage that the Laws of the Game allow him in order to claim those crosses within his range. Of course there will be the odd error of judgement, or days when conditions are not conducive to good handling. However, he must be mentally tough and demonstrate complete faith in his ability to deal effectively with the situation.

On those occasions when confidence is low, he must convince himself that as he has taken hundreds of crosses in the past he can do it again. Furthermore, a shaky, hesitant goalkeeper who does not accept his responsibilities will unsettle defenders and inspire opponents.

There are several stages in dealing with crosses.

- Starting position.

- Communication with the defence.

- Assessing the flight and the pace of the ball.

- Decision-making – to come or stay.

- Communicating the decision.

- The technique of dealing with the cross – catch, punch or deflect.

STARTING POSITION

When the ball is wide and about to be crossed, the goalkeeper's starting position is critical, since a yard either way can mean the difference between being close enough to attack the ball or being out of range. If the ball is wide, the keeper should start from a position slightly behind the centre of the goal. The reason for this is that it is easier to take the ball moving forwards than backwards. A keeper starting too close to the near post will be struggling to deal with a deep cross. As the ball carrier nears the goal, the keeper should move towards his near post to cover a possible shot. (See Figures 23 and 24.)

The keeper's starting position is also related to the proximity of the crosser. The further the crosser is from the goal area, the greater the distance the keeper should be from his goal line. This advanced starting position will extend his range and thereby increase his effectiveness. (See photo 50.)

Photo 50

The keeper should also adopt an open stance. This serves three purposes.

- He is in a good position to move rapidly forwards if the situation demands.

- He is facing play if a cross is whipped in and he has to make a reaction save.

- It allows him to be aware of the movement of opponents behind him. A closed body position denies him this fuller field of vision.

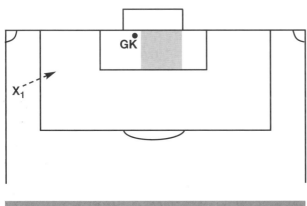

Figure 23 Incorrect starting position

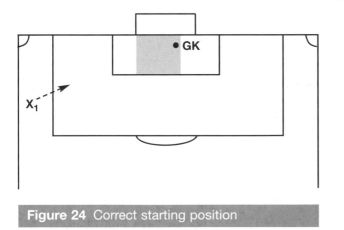

Figure 24 Correct starting position

COMMUNICATION WITH THE DEFENCE

The goalkeeper can make the job of dealing with crosses easier by creating space for himself. By discouraging his fellow defenders from dropping too deep around him, he will force opponents to take up positions away from the goal. In other words, if he instructs his team-mates to hold their line at the edge of the penalty area, the opposition will not be able to make early runs into the danger area for fear of being offside.

The point at which the defence holds its line will depend on the position of the ball. Generally, the further the ball is from the goal the higher the line. If executed effectively, the keeper will create space for himself in which he can attack the ball under minimal pressure (see the shaded area in Figure 25). Furthermore, if the opponent does connect with the cross, the header or shot is delivered from a safer distance.

The goalkeeper is in the best position to make the decision of where to hold the line. Teams should practise defending the penalty area in training and agree upon certain responses to a range of given situations. The goalkeeper, through a loud call, should communicate the response. This should be brief (such as 'Up to the spot' or 'Hold the edge') and clearly understood by his colleagues.

There are four prerequisites for effectively holding the line.

- The crosser must always be put under pressure to reduce the quality of the cross.

- The line should not leave too much space for the keeper to deal with.

- All defending players must move as one to form a uniform line.

- The keeper should take up an advanced position ready to attack the ball when it is delivered in behind the defence.

It is recommended that the goalkeeper understands where to hold the line. There are five easy points of reference.

- The 'D'.

- The edge of the penalty area.

- The penalty spot.

- The 6-yard line.

- Level with the ball.

Generally speaking, if the ball is cleared or passed towards the opponents' goal, the defence should look to move out to compress play. The extent of this movement will depend on the length of the clearance or pass. If the clearance falls to a team-mate or forces the opposition to turn and chase the ball, the defence can push up quickly to condense play. However, if the clearance drops to an opponent and there is a danger of the ball being rebounded behind the defence, the defenders should only move out gradually with pressure being applied to the ball carrier.

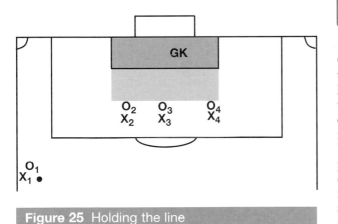

Figure 25 Holding the line

ASSESSING THE FLIGHT AND THE PACE OF THE BALL

Although it sounds obvious, the goalkeeper must assess the ball's flight and pace before moving. The many distractions around him, such as his defenders, opponents and his own expectations of where he thinks the ball will be played, will tempt him to anticipate the cross. This type of gambling can prove disastrous. Indeed, the most common cause of a keeper missing a cross is that he moves his feet before reading its flight and pace. He must treat every cross on its own merit and not commit himself before the ball is kicked.

Generally, for crosses that are driven in, the keeper must move fast and win the race to the ball. For crosses floated in, he must arrive late so that he is not caught underneath the ball. By making his attack at the last possible moment, he will be able to use a running jump and, as he will be aware of the players challenging him, his decision to catch or punch will be more reliable.

DECISION-MAKING

Having assessed the flight of the ball, the keeper must elect to either stay on his line or to attack the ball. This decision is based on the ball's trajectory, pace and distance from the goal line, as well as the proximity of other players. If, in the keeper's judgement, he has sufficient time to deal safely with the situation, then he should come for the cross. If he has decided not to go for the cross, the keeper should remain on his line and not be drawn to the ball. By stepping back to the line, the keeper might 'buy' himself that extra split-second in which to make a reaction save. In following the ball, the keeper can be caught in 'no man's land' and be vulnerable to the looping header beyond him. For crosses driven into the near post area, the goalkeeper should move quickly to cover the front half of the goal as this is the likely destination of a quick snap shot or header.

After electing to come for the cross, it is essential that the keeper makes contact with the ball. From the time he decides to go for the cross, his intention must be to catch the ball because that will effectively end the attack. However, at the last moment he must re-appraise the situation and decide whether to catch, punch or deflect the ball. This decision is based on how confident the keeper is of making a safe catch.

If the pressure from opponents between the keeper and the ball makes safe handling unlikely, then the keeper should attempt to punch the ball. When the ball is swinging in towards the cross-bar, making catching difficult, the keeper should deflect it over the bar for a corner. Similarly, if the goalkeeper is back-pedalling beyond the back post and cannot reach the ball with two hands, he should palm the ball to safety.

COMMUNICATING THE DECISION

The keeper should communicate with his defenders every time the ball is played into the penalty area. As far as crosses are concerned, if the keeper decides to come he should call 'Keeper's!' and if he elects to stay he should call 'Away!'. The keeper should call early so that his team-mates have time to react. A late call can confuse players who are already committed to a course of action.

In addition, the way in which the keeper communicates is important. His calls must be loud, clear and positive. Defenders will be unsettled by hesitant or panic-stricken instructions. The keeper must give the impression that he is calm and in control of the situation. A good confident call is often the prelude to a good confident catch. A keeper who exudes confidence will inspire and set the tone for the rest of the defence.

THE TECHNIQUE OF DEALING WITH THE CROSS

Having assessed the flight, decided to come for the cross and then communicated his intention to team-mates, the keeper must look to gather the ball at the highest possible point. By not attacking the ball there is a danger of opponents getting to it first. Some goalkeepers make the mistake of moving perpendicularly from the line to the cross instead of moving diagonally into the flight of the ball to take it earlier and at the highest point. (See Figure 26.)

With the benefit of a good starting position, more often than not, the keeper will take the cross moving forwards. He should take off from one foot, bringing up the other leg to give extra lift and some protection against opponents' challenges. If a cross is a deep one, the keeper should move backwards quickly using little mincing steps before taking off from one foot.

Catching

The goalkeeper must always expect to be challenged when moving out to collect a cross. In this way he will brace his body for physical contact and not be taken by surprise when it occurs. He should avoid locking out the arms when catching as the ball will be easily dislodged under an aggressive challenge. Catching the ball with arms slightly bent affords a much stronger grip.

Photo 51

It goes without saying that a catch is preferable to a punch, but the keeper must weigh up the risk factor and choose the safer option.

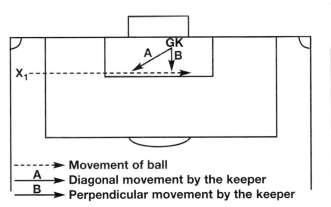

Movement of ball

A → Diagonal movement by the keeper

B → Perpendicular movement by the keeper

Figure 26 Attacking the cross

It is recommended that the goalkeeper makes his catch in front of the body and above the head. This serves three purposes.

- It allows him to see the ball into his hands.

- By using his arms as shock absorbers, it provides some margin for error if any mishandling occurs.

- It offers greater leverage if at the last moment he decides to punch. (See photo 51.)

Punching

If the decision is to punch, then the keeper must aim for height, distance and width. When combined, these factors give defenders time to deal with the next wave of attack. Ideally, the keeper should look to punch the ball out of the danger area. For balls swinging in towards the keeper, a punch should be made with two hands because this provides more reliable contact. (See photo 52.)

Photo 52

Although using one fist will provide greater reach and may be necessary in emergencies, it can result in a poor connection because the striking surface is narrow and often the keeper is hitting across the body. One-handed punches are more appropriate than the double-fisted clearance when the ball is moving away from the keeper. (See photo 53.)

In order to achieve maximum height and distance in his punch, the keeper should use the flat part of the fist and strike through the bottom half of the ball. The movement should be more of a jab than a swing. He should avoid clenching the fist too tightly as this makes the striking surface uneven and will result in a mistimed punch. By keeping the wrists rigid it will be possible to transfer maximum power from the forearms into the punch.

Photo 53

Deflecting

If the ball is swinging in dangerously close to the cross-bar and a safe catch is unlikely, the keeper should attempt to turn the ball over the bar using the open hand further from the goal line. An open hand affords greater reach than a fist and the fingers are more sensitive than knuckles. Using the arm further away from the goal line allows the keeper greater reach and is more comfortable as the wrist rotates forwards rather than backwards. However, in emergencies the keeper may not have the time or space to execute this skill in textbook fashion and may have to use the hand closer to the goal line.

The same open-handed technique is recommended when the keeper is back-pedalling beyond the back post and is unable to catch the ball. The ball should be deflected over the line for a corner.

Once committed to the cross it is absolutely imperative that the keeper makes contact with the ball. At best, the goalkeeper should catch and, at worst, he should try to alter the flight path of the ball. Opponents coming in behind the keeper will be following the path of the ball and a deflection might distract them and prevent a clean header.

Since collecting a high cross is an advanced skill, coaches should not expect perfect catches from young boys and girls. Most children below the age of 12 do not possess the hand size or strength to catch a high ball. Therefore it is quite acceptable for goalkeepers of that age to parry the ball first and to follow up quickly with a second save.

(1) CATCHING A HIGH BALL MOVING FORWARDS

Organisation

From a distance of 10 yards the server throws the ball high into the air so that the keeper moves forwards to catch it.

Key points

- Assess the flight and pace of the ball.

- Take off on one foot.

- Catch the ball on the way up.

- Take the ball at the highest point so that it is in front of the eye-line (using the 'W' hand shape and the forearms as shock absorbers).

- Bring the ball back into the chest.

(2) CATCHING A HIGH BALL MOVING BACKWARDS

Organisation

From a distance of 6 yards the server feeds the ball over the keeper's head so that he has to move quickly backwards to make the catch. The keeper should practise moving backwards using a sideways glide as well as square-on.

Key points

- Assess the flight and pace of the ball.

- Take quick, mincing steps backwards.

- Take off from one foot.

- Catch the ball at the highest point so that it is in front of the eye-line (using the 'W' hand shape and the forearms as shock absorbers).

- Bring the ball back into the chest.

- Go to ground if off-balance.

(3) CATCHING THE BALL TAKING OFF FROM BOTH FEET

Organisation

This practice attempts to re-create the situation when the keeper is caught underneath the ball and is forced into a two-foot take-off. The server stands by the side of the goalkeeper and throws the ball directly up into the air. The keeper has to take off from where he stands to catch the ball. Progress to the server challenging the keeper as he goes to catch.

Key points

- Assess the flight of the ball.

- Take off from two feet.

- Catch the ball on the way up.

- Catch the ball at the highest point (using the 'W' hand shape and forearms as shock absorbers).

- Brace the body for a challenge.

- Bring the ball back into the chest.

(4) BASKETBALL

Organisation

This practice is designed to prepare the keeper for the physical challenges he can expect in a game situation. The practice can take the form of a 2 v 2 or 3 v 3 in a grid measuring 15 yards x 15 yards. Each team must keep possession via throws passed above head height. Five consecutive passes caught above head height constitute a goal. The participants are not allowed to run with the ball or prevent an opponent from passing. Possession may only be gained via an interception.

Key points

- Assess the flight and pace of the ball.

- Catch the ball at the highest point (using the 'W' hand shape and forearms as shock absorbers).

- Brace the body for a challenge.

- Bring the ball back into the chest.

(5) CATCHING A BALL DELIVERED FROM THE SIDE

Organisation

The server stands at the junction of the 6-yard box and throws the ball across the face of the goal. The service is varied so that the keeper takes some balls going forwards and others going backwards.

Key points

- Adopt a good starting position (backwards from centre).

- Take up a sideways stance.

- Assess the flight of the ball.

- Take off on one foot.

- Catch the ball on the way up.

- Take the ball at the highest point (using the 'W' hand shape and forearms as shock absorbers).

- Bring the ball back into the chest.

(6) CATCH OR PUNCH

Organisation

As in (5) but an opponent challenges for the ball. The server varies the trajectory and pace of the ball so that the keeper has to decide whether to catch or punch. Progress to head-on service. (See photos 54a and 54b.)

Key points

- Adopt a good starting position (backwards from centre).

- Take up a sideways stance.

- Assess the flight (react to the ball, not to the movement of the opponent).

- Take off from one foot to take the ball at the highest point.

- If the trajectory is low, win the race to the ball. If the ball is hung up, go late.

- Brace the body for a challenge.

- Decide whether to catch or punch at the last moment.

- Use the 'W' hand shape and forearms as shock absorbers if looking to catch.

Photo 54a Photo 54b

- If punching, aim for height, distance and width. Use two hands for the inswinging ball and one hand for the ball across the body.

(7) DEALING WITH CROSSES WITHOUT OPPOSITION

Organisation

Having dealt effectively with hand service, it is now appropriate to move to a more realistic practice where crosses are kicked in. The novice keeper will initially experience problems because catching properly delivered crosses is much more difficult than dealing with thrown balls. The server crosses the ball from a wide position and the keeper comes to collect the cross.

Key points

- Adopt a good starting position (backwards of centre and off the line in relation to the position of the ball).

- Take up a sideways stance.

- Assess the flight and pace of the ball.

- Take off on one foot.

- Take the ball on the way up.

- Catch the ball at the highest point (using the 'W' hand shape and forearms as shock absorbers).

- Bring the ball back into the chest.

(8) DEALING WITH CROSSES WITH A DEFENDER IN ATTENDANCE

Organisation

As in (7), but a defender is introduced.

Key points

- Adopt a good starting position (as in (7)).

- Take up a sideways stance.

- Instruct the defender where to stand.

- Assess the flight and pace of the ball.

- Decide whether to attack the ball or to stay.

- Communicate the decision – 'Keeper's!' or 'Away!'.

- If staying, get back on the line. If coming, take the ball at the highest point on the way up.

- Use the 'W' hand shape and the forearms as shock absorbers.

- Bring the ball back into the chest.

(9) DEALING WITH CROSSES WITH TWO DEFENDERS AND ONE ATTACKER IN ATTENDANCE

Organisation

Similar to (8), but the keeper is assisted by two defenders and opposed by one attacker. As the goalkeeper gains in confidence more players can be added. Throughout the practice, the server crosses from wide positions with a variety of delivery angles. Occasionally he may set the ball back to a supporting player who crosses from a new position. This will force the keeper to push out the defenders. (See Figure 27.)

Key points

- Adopt a good starting position (backwards from centre and off the line in relation to the position of the ball).

- Take up a sideways stance.

- Do not allow defenders to drop too deep unless the crosser is close to the goal line. Get them to hold a line.

- Assess the flight and pace of the ball.

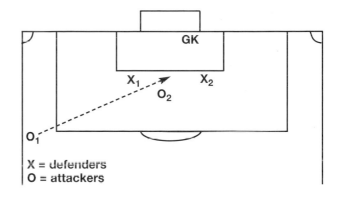

X = defenders
O = attackers

Figure 27 Dealing with crosses in practice

- Decide whether to attack the ball or stay.

- Communicate the decision – 'Keeper's!' or 'Away!'.

- If staying, move back to the line and prepare for a shot or header. If coming, take the ball at the highest point on the way up.

- Decide whether to catch, punch or deflect to safety.

- Apply the appropriate technique.

- The nearest defender should offer protection by occupying the space between the keeper and the attacker.

- The second defender should cover the line.

(10) DEALING WITH CROSSES IN A SMALL-SIDED GAME

Organisation

The practice takes the form of a small-sided game (four against four with two wingers and two goalkeepers) in an area 50 yards x 60 yards. The players, who are not allowed past the halfway line, are arranged into two attackers versus two defenders in each half. The two wingers are 'floaters' who support the team in possession and are allowed to move unchallenged up and down a 5-yard channel. The goalkeeper, or any one of the outfield players, passes the ball to the winger who makes ground before crossing into the opponent's goal-mouth. Offsides apply (See Figure 28.) Progress to introducing more players in each half.

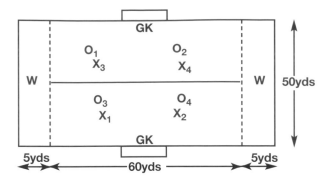

Key points
- Adopt a good starting position.
- Good communication.
- Good decision-making.
- Good technique.
- Defenders offer protection and cover the line.
- Good distribution.

(11) HELPING ON

Organisation

The goalkeeper sits on the ground while the server, from a distance of between 4 and 6 yards, throws the ball over the keeper's head. The keeper has to help the ball on to another server standing 3 yards behind. The service should almost be out of reach so that the keeper is unable to make a clean catch. (See photo 55.)

Key points
- Assess the flight of the ball.
- Catch the ball if possible.
- If helping the ball on, use the fingers to alter its flight.
- Practise using the open and closed hand techniques.

(12) TURNING THE BALL OVER THE CROSS-BAR

Organisation

The goalkeeper positions himself ready for a cross. The server, standing at the junction of the 6-yard box and the goal line, throws the ball towards the cross-bar. (See photo 56.)

Key points
- Adopt a good starting position.
- Take up a sideways stance.
- Assess the flight and pace of the ball.
- Decide whether to catch or deflect the ball over the bar.
- Turn the ball over the bar using the hand further away from the goal line.

(13) PUNCHING

Organisation

The goalkeeper sits facing the server who feeds the ball from a distance of 2 or 3 yards to the keeper's right hand. He punches the ball back, aiming for the server's chest. The keeper punches 10 times with the right hand, 10 times with the left hand, and 10 times with both.

Photo 55   Photo 56

Key points

- Keep the wrist rigid.

- Make contact with the flat part of the fist.

- Jab straight through the bottom half of the ball.

- Follow straight through.

(14) PUNCHING IN A LYING POSITION
Organisation

The keeper lies in the prone position facing the server, who positions himself a yard away. The server feeds the ball to the keeper's right hand and he punches the ball back. The goalkeeper looks to achieve height in the punch. The serving schedule is the same as for (13). (See photo 57.)

Key points
As in (13).

(15) PUNCHING OFF-BALANCE
Organisation

As in (13), but the direction and pace of service is varied and more challenging. The keeper has to decide whether to use two fists or one. By varying the service the keeper may have to punch while off-balance. (See photo 58.)

Key points

- Keep the wrists rigid.

- Make contact with the flat part of the wrist.

- Jab straight through the bottom half of the ball.

- Follow straight through.

- Be prepared to improvise with the heel of the hand if it is not possible to get the fist under the ball.

Photo 57

Photo 58

DISTRIBUTION 11

If the goalkeeper is the last line of defence he is, by implication, the first line of attack

Since the goalkeeper has possession of the ball more than any other player, it is imperative that he uses it well. It is infuriating to see a keeper having made a fine catch, surrender possession through a careless throw or kick. Indeed often at the moment the keeper makes a save, the opposition is at its most vulnerable in terms of a counter attack. With six seconds and the whole of the penalty area at his disposal, speedy and incisive distribution can have devastating results.

The manner in which the coach instructs his goalkeeper to distribute the ball will form the basis for the team's pattern of play. Some coaches will encourage their goalkeeper to throw the ball at every opportunity so that play can be built from the back. Others will prefer their keepers to miss out the defence and midfield by kicking deep into enemy territory in order to maximise his own team's strengths and/or to exploit the weaknesses of his opponents.

With such a heavy responsibility, the goalkeeper should constantly practise throwing and kicking techniques so that his distribution becomes an asset rather than a liability to the team. Since he has to take more free kicks (for offsides and goal kicks mostly) than any other player, it is essential that he is one of the most proficient dead-ball kickers in the team. It is not sufficient to be able to kick the ball over a great distance, he must do it accurately and consistently. If the keeper is reliable with his kicks, the team can then adapt their tactics accordingly. However, if a goalkeeper's distribution is erratic, his kicking will take on a negative rather than a positive connotation.

Throws are generally quicker and more accurate than kicks, and the keeper can use them to guarantee his team retains possession. It is important, therefore, that a ball thrown by the goalkeeper does not give the recipient a control problem. If the recipient has to waste precious seconds in controlling the ball, it defeats the whole object of the exercise.

Having mastered the techniques of throwing and kicking, the keeper must develop an understanding of when and where to use them. As soon as the goalkeeper collects the ball he must move forward quickly holding the ball in front of him primed and ready for a throw or kick. When moving forward the goalkeeper should be scanning the whole pitch looking for the opportunity to exploit the opposition who may be weak defensively. Counter attacking is all about speed of thought, movement and ball. The good goalkeeper will quickly assess the situation and identify the following:

- Areas where the opposition's defensive arrangement is vulnerable (for example no covering defenders at the back of the defence).

- The options available to him (for example kicking quickly into the opponent's half or switching play with a fast throw to the opposite flank).

- His team-mates' strengths (for example his most forward player may have great pace and would benefit from a ball hit behind the opposition's defence).

- The most appropriate method of distribution

On a cautionary note, however, the goalkeeper should not be thinking about the throw before making the save. Many keepers have been embarrassed because they have taken their eye off the ball at the last minute.

The goalkeeper's distribution should not put his own goal under immediate threat. An understanding of risk assessment will help the keeper to make sensible selections. With a wayward kick into the opponent's half, his team has half of the field to regain possession, whereas a risky short throw to a team-mate can spell disaster. He must not pass the ball to colleagues in his own half when there is little chance of their retaining possession.

Sometimes the state of play will dictate how the keeper distributes. If his team is under severe pressure, the goalkeeper is advised to take the heat out of the situation by playing the ball out with his feet. Of course, this can only be attempted when there are no opponents in the vicinity. He should also be able to assess the strengths and weaknesses of the opposition and distribute the ball accordingly. For instance, it would be futile persisting with high clearances when his own forwards are dwarfed by the opposing defenders. As all opponents are different and pose varying problems and challenges, it is important that teams are adaptable when it comes to receiving the ball from the goalkeeper. Coaches who neglect working on distribution from the keeper do so at their own peril.

THROWING TECHNIQUES

The roll

The roll is used for very short distances, usually to pass to defenders on the edge of the penalty area.

Photo 59c

Photo 59d

The actual technique is similar to the ten pin bowling action where the ball is kept in contact with the ground for as long as possible. The keeper can achieve this by keeping low and following through on the roll. (See photos 59a, 59b, 59c and 59d.)

The javelin throw

This is used for slightly longer distances and involves a whiplash action which resembles throwing a javelin. By flicking the wrist on delivery, slice will be imparted to the ball, thus keeping the bounce low. The risk of giving the receiver a difficult bouncing ball will be further reduced if the keeper stays low throughout the delivery. Ideally, the ball should reach the recipient below knee height. (See photo 60.)

Photo 59a

Photo 59b

Photo 60

Photo 61a

Photo 61b

Photo 61c

Photo 61d

The overarm throw

If performed well and employed at the appropriate moment, this throw can be a potent attacking weapon because it can play several opponents out of the game at one time. It is used to cover distances beyond which the keeper would have to kick. It is often employed when the opposition have committed numbers in attack and the goalkeeper tries to catch them on the break. These throws are more effective when kept low because they take less time to reach their intended target. However, when opponents are blocking the direct route, the ball has to spend most of its journey airborne.

The actual technique is a bowling action whereby the goalkeeper takes the ball back with a fairly straight arm and follows through quite vigorously. The point of release depends on how much air the keeper intends to give the ball. If he is looking to clear players, then an early release is recommended, but if there are no obstacles between himself and his target, not only can he release the ball late, but he can also impart slice in order to keep it low. (See photos 61a, 61b, 61c, 61d and 61e.)

KICKING TECHNIQUES

Goal kicks

Goalkeepers who consistently achieve distance and accuracy from their dead-ball kicks will prove an asset to the team. It is demoralising for a team to be regularly put on the defensive by its keeper's weak

kicking. However, even though he fails to clear any great distance, the keeper can save the day if he can kick accurately to strategically placed team-mates. The coach should be aware of his goalkeeper's strengths and weaknesses in this department and should implement an appropriate pattern of play. If the keeper consistently kicks long, he can push players well forward into the opponent's half since players cannot be

Photo 61e

offside from a goal kick. But, if the keeper repeatedly fails to reach the halfway line, the target players can drop deeper in order to win the first touch.

Coaches of school and youth teams should persevere with their goalkeepers even if their goal kicks are poor. Players at this level are at a crucial stage of their development and should not be denied learning experiences such as taking goal kicks. If the keeper is not permitted to take his own goal kicks there will be little motivation for him to improve his technique. Moreover, having an outfield player taking goal kicks encourages the opposing strikers to push forwards in the knowledge that they will not be offside if the ball is returned by their midfield or defence.

If the coach is concerned about the lack of distance achieved by his young keeper's kicks, he should strategically place defenders in the penalty area so that opponents gaining possession are immediately put under pressure. According to the Laws of the Game, opponents must take up positions outside the penalty area, whereas the team taking the goal kick can go where they please.

Regardless of whether or not the keeper is a good dead-ball kicker, he must think twice about aiming across the field. If the kick falls short he may be caught out of position with very little time to recover. To be safe he should aim his kicks to the same side of the field.

The volley

The volley is the more common method used when kicking from the hands. The advantages of the volley are that the ball can be passed over considerable distances and it is fairly reliable. With the volley and half-volley techniques the keeper should drop rather than toss up the ball before striking it. The longer the ball is in the air, especially in windy conditions, the greater the chances of a poor kick. By almost placing the ball on to the foot the goalkeeper can improve the quality of the contact and, in turn, increase the reliability of his kicks.

The half-volley

If executed well, the half-volley is a more effective technique than the volley because its lower trajectory results in the ball reaching its target in a shorter time. It is useful when playing into a strong wind or when there is an opportunity for a quick counter-attack. However, care must be taken when playing on muddy or bumpy grounds because good contact with the ball cannot be guaranteed. With this in mind it is not recommended to attempt this technique in the 6-yard area.

Kicks from the ground

If it is safe to do so the goalkeeper may elect to drop the ball and, rather than clear from the hands, kick from the ground.

Kicks from the ground can serve four purposes.

- It can 'buy' the defence time, especially when the team is under pressure.

- The keeper can move the ball beyond the edge of the area to achieve greater distance on the clearance.

- Kicking from the ground results in a lower trajectory and is generally more accurate than the volley method.

- It is easier to kick from the ground when facing a strong breeze.

Kicking from the ground is not advisable when opponents are nearby, or if conditions are heavy and it is not easy to achieve elevation on the ball.

(1) THE ROLL TO A STATIONARY TARGET
Organisation
The keeper rolls the ball to a receiver standing 6–10 yards away. The receiver controls and then returns the ball.

Key points
- Point the leading foot in the direction of the target.

- Use a ten pin bowling action.

- Keep low.

- Ensure a good follow-through.

- Do not give the receiver control problems – keep the ball low.

(2) THE ROLL TO A MOVING TARGET
Organisation
As in (1), but on the command the receiver sets off at an angle and the keeper has to find him with a rolled pass.

Key points
- Point the front foot in the direction of the target.

- Keep low.

- Ensure a good follow-through.

- Aim slightly in front of the receiver so that he does not have to check his stride.

- Keep the ball low so that the receiver does not have a control problem.

(3) THE JAVELIN THROW TO A STATIONARY TARGET

Organisation

The keeper uses the javelin throw to pass to a receiver standing 10–15 yards away. The receiver controls and then returns the ball.

Key points

- Point the front foot and non-throwing arm in the direction of the target.

- Keep low.

- Use a javelin arm action.

- Flick the wrist on delivery to impart slice to the ball.

- Keep the ball low so that the receiver does not have a control problem.

(4) THE JAVELIN THROW TO A MOVING TARGET

Organisation

As for (3), but on the command the receiver sets off at an angle and the keeper has to pass to him using a javelin throw.

Key points

- Point the front foot and non-throwing arm in the direction of the target.

- Keep low.

- Use a javelin arm action.

- Flick the wrist on delivery to impart slice to the ball.

- Aim slightly in front of the receiver so that he does not have to check his stride.

- Keep the ball low so that it does not present a control problem for the receiver.

(5) THE OVERARM THROW TO A STATIONARY TARGET

Organisation

The keeper throws the ball using the overarm technique to a target 15–35 yards away. The receiver controls and then returns the ball.

Key points

- Point the leading foot and non-throwing arm towards the target.

- Ensure a straight arm preparation.

- Use a fast follow-through and a late release.

- Flick wrist on delivery to impart slice to the ball.

- Keep the ball low so that the receiver is not presented with a control problem.

(6) THE OVERARM THROW – CLEARING AN OPPONENT

Organisation

As for (5), but an opponent stands in the line of flight so that the keeper has to clear him to find his target.

Key points

- Point the leading foot and non-throwing arm towards the target.

- Ensure a straight arm preparation.

- Use a slow follow-through with an early release.

- Aim to drop the ball at the receiver's feet.

(7) THE OVERARM THROW TO A MOVING TARGET

Organisation

As for (5), but on the command the receiver sets off at an angle and the keeper has to find him using an overarm throw.

Key points

- Point the leading foot and non-throwing arm towards the target.

- Ensure a straight arm preparation.

- Use a fast follow-through with a late release.

- Flick the wrist on delivery to impart slice to the ball.

- Aim slightly in front of the receiver so that he does not have to check his stride.

- Keep the ball low so that the receiver is not presented with a control problem.

(8) THE OVERARM THROW TO A MOVING TARGET – CLEARING AN OPPONENT

Organisation
As for (6), but the receiver sets off at an angle and the keeper has to clear the opponent to find his team-mate.

Key points

- Point the leading foot and non-throwing arm towards the target.

- Ensure a straight arm preparation.

- Use a slow follow-through with an early release.

- Aim to drop the ball at the receiver's feet so that he does not have to check his stride.

(9) THE GOAL KICK

Organisation
The keeper kicks the ball over four 10-yard grids to a target player. (See Figure 29.) As the goalkeeper becomes proficient, extend the target range by one set of grids so that the keeper is kicking over 50 yards. If two goalkeepers are working at the same task a competition could by organised with the winner being the first to complete ten successful kicks. To achieve a successful kick the ball has to reach the final grid without bouncing. (See photos 62a and 62b.)

Photo 62a   Photo 62b

Key points

- Check the position of the target.

- Make an angled approach – two o'clock position for a right-footed kick, ten o'clock position for a left-footed kick.

- The non-kicking foot should be positioned to the side and behind the ball.

- The kicking foot should be pointed outwards, with the ankle firm and extended.

- Contact should be made with the instep (laces) through the bottom half of the ball.

- The eyes should be looking down at the ball with the head steady.

- Ensure a smooth follow-through.

- Relax, don't try too hard.

When kicking against a strong wind, the keeper should aim for a lower trajectory by reducing the run-up and the angle of approach, and also by planting the non-kicking foot closer to the ball.

(10) THE ROLL-OUT KICK

Organisation
As for (9), but this time the goalkeeper drops the ball, plays the ball out of the feet, and kicks it to the target standing 40–50 yards away. Vary the distance to suit the needs of the players. Make it competitive – the winner is the first to do ten successful kicks.

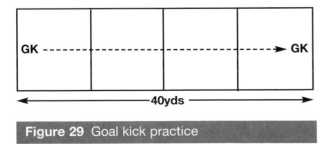

Figure 29 Goal kick practice

Key points

- Roll the ball out of the feet to the two o'clock position if right-footed or the ten o'clock position if left-footed.

- Check the position of the intended target.

- Ensure that the position of the ball allows a reasonable run-up.

- The non-kicking foot should be positioned to the side and behind the ball.

- The kicking foot should be pointed outwards, with the ankle firm and extended.

- Contact should be made with the instep (laces) through the bottom half of the ball.

- Ensure a relaxed and smooth follow-through.

- The eyes should be looking down at the ball, with the head steady.

(11) THE VOLLEY

Organisation
As for (10). Vary the distance to suit the needs of the players. (See photos 63a, 63b, 63c, 63d.)

Key points

- Hold the ball with two hands out in front of the body at waist height.

- Check the position of the intended target.

- Drop the ball on to the kicking foot.

- Using the instep (laces), strike the ball in front of the body.

- Place the non-kicking foot behind the line of the ball.

- Make contact through the middle of the ball.

- Ensure a smooth follow-through.

- Keep the head steady, with the eyes fixed on the ball.

- Relax, don't try too hard.

(12) VOLLEYING TO A VARIETY OF TARGETS

Organisation
The practice takes place on the pitch with a range of targets placed around the halfway line. Vary the distance to suit the ability of the players. So that progress can be monitored, points are awarded for an accurate volley.

Key points
As for (11).

Photo 63a

Photo 63b

Photo 63c

Photo 63d

(13) THE HALF-VOLLEY

Organisation

As for (11) and (12), but the goalkeeper half-volleys the ball to the receiver. (See photos 64a, 64b, 64c, 64d and 64e.)

Key points

- Check the position of the intended target.

- Hold the ball in two hands in front of the body at waist height.

- Drop the ball so that it pitches just in front of the non-kicking foot.

- Use the instep (laces) of the kicking foot, striking through the bottom half of the ball just as it hits the ground.

- Ensure a smooth follow-through, with the body leaning backwards.

- Keep the head steady, with the eyes fixed on the ball.

- Relax, don't try too hard.

To achieve a lower trajectory, the ball should be dropped closer to the non-kicking foot and contact should be made through the centre of the ball. The knee should be over the ball, with the body leaning forwards on the follow-through.

Photo 64a

Photo 64b

Photo 64c

Photo 64d

Photo 64e

(14) SCANNING

Organisation

This practice is designed to help the goalkeeper to select the best distribution option and to execute it effectively. The ball is played into the goal area where the keeper collects (see Figure 30). He then runs forward and has to choose from one of three targets. The coach moves to block off the passing lane to one of the targets. The object of the exercise is to choose the most penetrative option and to execute the most effective form of distribution with appropriate quality. The coach assesses the goalkeeper on three areas (i) correct decision (ii) most appropriate distribution method (iii) quality of distribution.

Key points

- After collecting, move forward scanning the options.

- Choose the most penetrative option.

- Choose the appropriate distribution method.

- Ensure quality distribution.

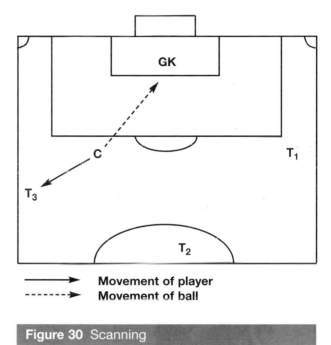

→ **Movement of player**
------→ **Movement of ball**

Figure 30 Scanning

Goalkeepers who are not comfortable with the back pass are a liability to their team

The law relating to the back pass means that the keeper has to be as comfortable with the ball at his feet as he is with it in his hands. This entails demonstrating good ball control as well as being proficient with both feet for long and short passes. Consequently, it is crucial that sufficient time is set aside to master and then polish these techniques. Warm-ups and cool-downs present the ideal times for this type of practise.

> Players pass the ball back to their goalkeeper for the following reasons.
>
> - As an emergency measure when they have nowhere else to go.
>
> - They cannot pass forward themselves.
>
> - To 'buy' the team some time.
>
> - To provide a point through which the team can switch the direction of play.
>
> - To maintain possession of the ball.

This means that the goalkeeper will not only have to make effective clearances under pressure, but also display the composure to control and pass the ball accurately when time and space is available.

One principle should dominate the goalkeeper's approach to dealing with back passes – **safety**. Since he is the last line of defence, he cannot afford to take risks, because one error of judgement can spell disaster. For this reason, he should avoid taking more touches than necessary and he should never attempt to dribble round an opponent. Memories of needlessly conceded goals because of a reckless attitude will haunt the goalkeeper for a long time. Instead the keeper should follow the age old maxim, 'if in doubt put it out'.

Dealing with the back pass involves two stages – preparation and distribution.

Preparation

ASSESSMENT
As play develops towards him the keeper has to identify that a back pass is a possibility and adopt an appropriate supporting position.

DISTANCE OF SUPPORT
The goalkeeper must leave sufficient space for his team-mate to pass the ball to him. If he takes up a position too close to his colleague he will put unnecessary pressure on the pass and also leave himself little time to deal with it once it arrives.

ANGLE OF SUPPORT
As the keeper's primary task is to protect the goal he should not take up a position that leaves it wide open. It is recommended that he positions himself between the ball and the goal so that if his team-mate misdirects the back pass it does not result in disastrous consequences.

COMMUNICATION
An early call will help his team-mate decide that the back pass is the best option. Furthermore the intonation of his voice should convey the urgency of the situation. For example if his team-mate is under

severe pressure the keeper should shout **'Man on! Pass it back early!'** in an excited manner. On the other hand when his colleague is under minimal pressure his call should be calm and indicate that the situation is not an emergency.

Distribution

TIME AVAILABLE
The proximity of the nearest opponent will indicate to the goalkeeper how many touches he can safely take. Needless to say if the opponent is very close then the clearance should be made with one touch. If pressure on the ball is insignificant, then the keeper will have the time to control the ball before making an accurate pass.

DIRECTION OF THE PASS
The opponent's angle of approach will dictate where the keeper should play the pass. If the keeper clears too close to the opponent the ball may rebound off him into the empty net. For this reason the pass should be angled away from the opponent's line of approach. If taking more than one touch, the keeper's first touch should take him away from the opponent.

TYPE OF PASS
If the goalkeeper has sufficient time he should choose the controlling surface, relax on contact, play the ball out of his feet and then make the pass. However, if time and space are at a premium, he will have to make a first-time clearance. Often the surfaces of goal areas are uneven and the keeper must take care that a good contact is made with the ball. Height and distance on the clearance will provide time for the defence to recover, so the keeper must concentrate on striking through the bottom half of the ball. This is fairly easy to achieve when the ball comes from the side but when the back pass is made straight at the keeper's feet with very little room for a reasonable back-lift, he should use the side of the foot to lift the ball over the first line of opponents.

When passing over short distances, for example to the nearest full back, the keeper should overhit rather than underhit the pass. If the pass has insufficient weight it increases the possibility of an interception. On the other hand if the pass is too strong for the full back the worst that can happen is a throw-in conceded.

In order to cope with the full range of eventualities, the keeper should work on a range of unopposed and game-related activities aimed at developing technical proficiency with both feet.

His fellow defenders should also work with him to develop an understanding of relative strengths and weaknesses. If the back pass is made to the keeper's weaker foot or if he is under severe pressure, the team should concentrate on damage limitation and move in field to become more compact. This assumes that possession will be lost and the team should prepare to defend. On the other hand if the pass is made to the goalkeeper's stronger foot and he is under little pressure, the team should spread out and attempt to build an attack.

(1) CONTROLLING OUT OF THE FEET
Organisation
The keeper stands in a grid measuring 2 x 2 yards. From a distance of 10–15 yards the server plays the ball to the keeper who has to control the ball with one touch out of the square and pass back to the server (see Figure 31). Progress to controlling with one foot and passing with the other.

Key points
- Get into line.
- Control the ball out of the feet i.e. 2 o'clock for the right foot and 10 o'clock for the left foot.
- Firm accurate pass back to the server.

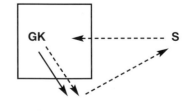

Figure 31 Controlling out of the feet

(2) ONE- OR TWO-TOUCH CONTROL
Organisation
From a distance of 10–15 yards the server plays the ball at various heights and speeds to the goalkeeper. As he releases the ball the server shouts 'One!' or 'Two!' and the keeper has to respond using the appropriate number of touches.

Key points
- Get into line.
- If two touches, select controlling surface.
- If one touch, ensure firm contact with foot, thigh or head.
- Relax on contact to play the ball out of the feet.
- Ensure a good quality pass on the second touch.

(3) PIGGY IN THE MIDDLE
Organisation
This practice takes place in a square 15 yards x 15 yards with a goalkeeper on each side. With a defender in the middle, the keepers on the outside have to keep possession without using their hands. Change the defender after every two minutes.

Key points
- Provide a passing angle for the man in possession.
- As the ball is on its way, quickly get into line.
- Decide on the number of touches to take.
- Control and pass away from the defender.

(4) SWITCHING PLAY
Organisation
Using the full width of the pitch Server 1 standing in the right back position, plays the ball to the goalkeeper who has to control across the body and pass to Server 2 standing in the left back position. (See Figure 32.) Progress to Server 3 putting pressure on the keeper so he has to decide on the number of touches and the direction of his pass.

Key points
- Take up a good supporting position.
- Adopt an open body position when receiving the ball.

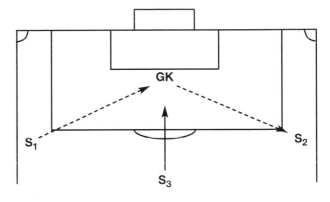

Figure 32 Switching play

- Be aware of the proximity of the nearest closing player.
- Control across the body.
- Pass accurately into the team mate's path.
- Overhit rather than underhit.

(5) 2 v 1 GAME
Organisation
This practice is designed to test the keeper's composure under pressure. In an area measuring 20 yards x 20 yards two outfield players exchange passes. Without warning, the ball is passed back to the goalkeeper. The passer then puts the goalkeeper under pressure while the other player makes an angle to receive the pass. (See Figure 33.)

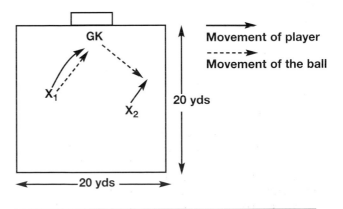

Figure 33 2 v 1 back pass game

Key points
- Get into line.
- Assess the proximity and the angle of approach of the opponent.
- Decide on the number of touches available.
- Control and pass away from the opponent.
- Team-mate should make a good passing angle.
- Support the pass.
- Do not take risks.

(6) LONG CLEARANCES
Organisation
This practice aims to help the goalkeeper to improve his ability to play long after receiving a back pass. The practice takes place over 40 x 10 yard grid with the keeper at one end and a target player T at the other (see Figure 34). The server (S) passes the ball to the keeper who has to clear the server and reach the target. The server varies his position and occasionally pressurises the pass so that the keeper has to clear first time.

Key points
- Get into line.
- Decide upon the appropriate number of touches.
- If two touch control out of the feet.
- Aim for height to clear the pressurising player.
- Do not take risks.

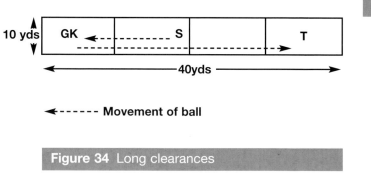

Figure 34 Long clearances

(7) LONG OR SHORT
Organisation
The practice is designed to assist the keeper in his decision making on whether to play long or short. It takes place over a 40 x 15 yard area with the goalkeeper in the end grid (see Figure 35). Server 1 plays the ball into the keeper at which point Server 2 pressurises the pass. The keeper has to choose whether to play short to Server 1, who has taken a supporting position, or long to the target player T.

Key points
- Get into line.
- Access the proximity and angle of approach of pressurising player.
- Decide on appropriate number of touches.
- Decide on target.
- If playing short overhit rather than underhit.
- If playing long aim for height to clear pressurising player.

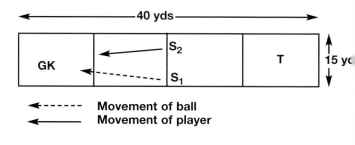

Figure 35 Long or short clearances

(8) BACK PASS UNDER PRESSURE

Organisation

The coach controls the service in this practice to meet the needs of his keeper. The practice takes place in the defensive half of the field with the coach serving the ball from the edge of the penalty area. On the coach's command an opponent pressurises the goalkeeper, who has to find one of two target players spread across the field. (See Figure 36.) The coach tests the goalkeeper's ability to deal with the pass by varying the service and the degree of pressure.

Key points

- Get into line.

- Assess the proximity and the angle of approach of the opponent.

- Decide on the number of touches available.

- If one touch, ensure good contact on the clearance. If more than one touch, control and pass away from the opponent.

- If passing long, aim for height and distance.

- Team-mates should make good passing angles.

- If appropriate, support the pass.

- Do not take risks.

(9) CONDITIONED SMALL-SIDED GAME

Organisation

This practice takes place in an area of 60 yards x 40 yards in a 7 v 7 game. The players are conditioned to pass back to the goalkeeper before the ball can cross the halfway line. The aims of the game are to practise dealing with the back pass under realistic conditions, and to develop an understanding with fellow defenders.

Key points

As for (8).

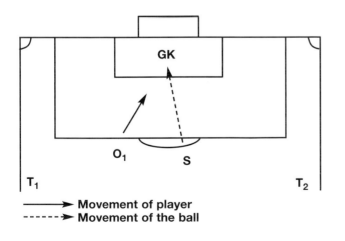

Figure 36 Back pass under pressure

SUPPORTING THE DEFENCE **13**

Even when the ball is far away from him the goalkeeper should live every second of the game and be ready to deal with any eventuality

As the last line of the defensive unit, the goalkeeper should not only be prepared to act as a sweeper if the ball is played over his defenders, but also as a passing option if his team has possession. Quick thinking and astute positioning can diffuse potentially dangerous situations. Allied to this positional responsibility is the work of the goalkeeper as a source of ongoing information. After all, he does enjoy a view of the whole pitch and is, therefore, perfectly placed to direct defensive operations.

There are five key factors in supporting the defence.

- Distance from the goal line.

- Distance from the rearmost defender.

- Communication with the defence.

- Assessment of the situation.

- Decision regarding the appropriate action.

- Positive action.

Distance from the goal line

The distance the goalkeeper should be from his own goal line varies according to the proximity of the ball. Obviously, his first priority is not to be beaten by a direct shot, but when the ball is some way from the goal the keeper should maintain the optimum

angle and distance so that he is ideally placed to intercept through-balls and assist team-mates who are in possession.

The following table may be used as a guide.

Location of the ball	Keeper's distance from the goal line
• In the opposition's penalty area.	18 yards
• Between the opposition's penalty area and the halfway line.	12–18 yards
• Between the halfway line and the arc of the centre circle.	6–10 yards
• Between the arc of the centre circle and the edge of the penalty area.	3–6 yards

Distance from the rearmost defender

All good defences are compact and the keeper should ensure that he does not become too detached from the rearmost defender. Skilful opponents will exploit large spaces left at the back of defences, so the goalkeeper should be aware of his sweeping role as play moves towards his goal.

> If the opponents do play a through ball, the well positioned keeper will be able to select the safest option from the following.
>
> - Leave the area and play to safety.
>
> - Wait until the ball reaches the penalty area and collect it.
>
> - Allow team-mates to give a clearance or make a back pass.
>
> Each of these options must be accompanied by an appropriate call.

If the keeper allows the team-mate to make a back pass he must take up a position that provides the passer with some margin of error. A pressurised colleague would rather pass over 6 yards than 1 or 2, so the goalkeeper must retreat to make the passing distance more appealing. The keeper must be prepared for the misdirected pass and not wander too far from the line of the posts. If the back pass is wayward, let it be at the expense of a corner and not an own goal. (See Figures 37 and 38.)

Communication

As the last line of the defence, the goalkeeper should use his excellent view of the whole field to direct defensive operations like the conductor of an orchestra. Whereas the conductor communicates with his baton, the goalkeeper uses his voice.

Goalkeepers who communicate well with fellow defenders are greatly valued. Clear, precise, early calls can alert team-mates to hitherto unforeseen dangers as well as averting any confusion. Also, constant communication with his defenders will aid the keeper's concentration, especially during those periods in the game when he is largely inactive.

> There are three elements to communication.
>
> - **When** – early so that team-mates have time to respond.
>
> - **What** – specific and succinct.
>
> - **How** – loud, clear and with authority.

WHEN

The timing of the communication is critical. The calls must be early enough for his team-mates to respond appropriately. Acting as the team's early warning system the keeper can nip potential danger in the bud by providing vital information. Whether it is a fairly straightforward call when advancing for a through ball, or a subtle adjustment to the shape of the defensive unit, it must be early. Late calls,

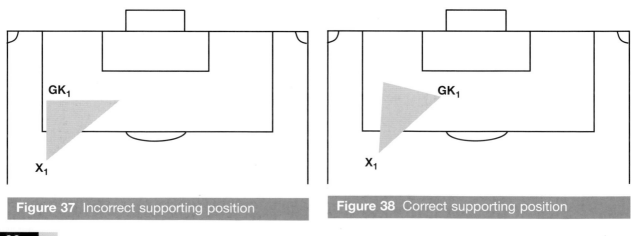

Figure 37 Incorrect supporting position

Figure 38 Correct supporting position

when team-mates are already committed to a course of action, can cause considerable confusion and significantly reduce the team's confidence in their keeper.

WHAT

It is important that the goalkeeper knows what to communicate. He should be fully conversant with his team's defensive strategy so that he can ensure that his team-mates adhere to the agreed tactics, both for set pieces and free play. He should not only be able to alert defenders to the movement of opponents, but also to provide useful information when his team has possession.

The vocabulary used by the keeper should be easily understood by his team-mates so that they can take the appropriate action. Communication should be short and unambiguous: precious seconds can be wasted by instructions that are long-winded and confusion caused by vague directions. The following goalkeeper's vocabulary might prove useful in supporting the defence.

WHEN IN POSSESSION

- When the team-mate has time on the ball:
  'Time – two-touch!'
  'Time, turn!'
  'Time, take it away!'

- When the team-mate has time and should switch play:
  'Time, switch it!'

- When the team-mate is under pressure:
  'Man on!'
  'Away, man on!'
  'Play it safe, man on!'

- When the keeper wants the ball-carrier to pass the ball back:
  'Keeper's on, push it back!'
  'Keeper's on, head it back!'

- When the keeper wants the player to leave the through-ball:
  'Keeper's, let it run/go!'

WHEN NOT IN POSSESSION

- When the keeper wants the team-mate to pressurise the ball-carrier:
  'Get tighter!'
  'Close him down quickly!'
  'Stay on your feet!'

- When the keeper wants to make play predictable:
  'Don't let him turn!'
  'Show him inside/down the line!'

- When the ball has been cleared and he wants the defence to make play compact:
  'Step up!' (If done gradually.)
  'Squeeze!' (If done quickly over a reasonable distance.)

- When the keeper wants the defence to hold a line:
  'Hold the edge!' (of the penalty area)
  'Hold the spot!'
  'Level with the 6!' (-yard box)
  'Level with the ball!'

It is worth making the distinction between 'stepping up' and 'squeezing up' when exhorting the defence to push up after making a clearance. The object of pushing up is not necessarily to catch opponents offside, but to make play compact and reduce the amount of space and time available to the opposition. If the clearance falls to an opponent, the defence should push out gradually and then only if the ball carrier is put under pressure. This is to prevent the opponents from rebounding the ball back into the danger area behind the defence. If the clearance forces the opposition to turn and chase the ball or falls to a team-mate in a forward position, the defence can push up quickly as there is little immediate danger of being caught out by an early pass to the back of the defence.

The purpose of holding the line is to make play compact and predictable but it cannot be done effectively unless the ball carrier is pressurised. The point at which the defence holds the line should make it difficult for the opponents to play a quality ball in behind the defence. Care must be taken that the line is not held too high as it will make it relatively easy for the opposition to play a penetrative pass. Whenever the defence holds the line, the keeper should be prepared to adopt an advanced starting position from which he can intercept passes played beyond it.

A word of caution. The keeper should never shout 'Leave it!' or 'Let it run!' without either prefixing it with the word 'Keeper's!' or by naming the team-mate involved, for example, 'Keeper's, let it run!' or 'Leave it, John!'. Failure to follow this advice could result in the referee penalising the goalkeeper for unsporting behaviour.

HOW

All information must be given in a loud, clear voice that instils confidence. Even if the goalkeeper feels nervous he should try to exude calmness. He will achieve this if he provides early and relevant information in a confident and controlled manner. The gravity of the situation will determine the intonation of the instruction. For example, the call of 'Man on!' should convey urgency whereas 'Time, two-touch!' should induce composure on the part of the team-mate.

The keeper should not forget to congratulate colleagues when they have performed well, but lambasting defenders is rarely beneficial and in fact probably disrupts concentration.

> In dealing with a through ball the keeper will be faced with one of the following permutations.
>
> - Will the ball reach the penalty area for him to collect?
>
> - Will he have to leave the penalty area to make a clearance?
>
> - Are defenders better placed to deal with the situation and should he take up a supporting position ready to receive a back pass?
>
> - Is the opponent clear of the defence with good control of the ball?

Assessment of the situation

Having taken up a good supporting position, the keeper will have to consider the scene in front of him and make a judgement on the most appropriate course of action.

Decision regarding appropriate action

It is important that the goalkeeper chooses wisely because an impetuous advance could gift a goal to the opposition, or an ill-judged challenge could result in a free kick or penalty being awarded followed by dismissal from the field of play. Having made the decision, he should communicate his intentions to his fellow defenders.

Positive action

Communication should be followed by positive action. The keeper cannot afford a moment's hesitation because there may be very little time available. If he decides to attack the ball he must make contact with it and clear the immediate threat. If he elects to hold his ground he must prepare himself for a shot or back pass. He must never get caught in two minds and leave himself in 'no man's land'. There will be occasions when he will make the wrong decision, but if his subsequent action is positive at least he will give his team a reasonable chance of averting the danger.

(1) SUPPORTING THE DEFENCE IN A SMALL-SIDED GAME

Organisation

This practice takes the form of 6 v 6 plus two goalkeepers in an area measuring 70 yards x 50 yards. The teams line up with two defenders, two midfielders and two strikers. The coach should set up the following starting points to provide the keeper and his defence with realistic practice.

- The goalkeeper's defence push up to the halfway line and the opposition's right back plays a straight ball down the flank into the back of the defence.

- The goalkeeper's centre back heads the ball weakly into the midfield area where it is played over his head into the space behind the defence.

- The opposition midfield plays into the feet of a striker who lays the ball off for a through-ball into the back of the defence.

Key points

- Adopt a good starting position relative to the goal line and the ball.

- Keep in line with the ball.

- Stay compact with the rearmost defender.

- Provide information for defensive players.

- Decide what course of action to take.

- Communicate the decision to team mates.

- Take positive action.

(2) SUPPORTING THE DEFENCE IN AN ATTACK v DEFENCE

Organisation

This practice takes place in one half of the field where there is an 8 v 8 situation. The attackers have to score past the goalkeeper whereas the defenders have to pass the ball through one of two targets either side of the centre circle to register a goal. Each practice is started by a ball being played into the space between the goalkeeper and the rearmost defender.

Key points

- Adopt a good starting position.

- Stay compact with the rearmost defender.

- Support team-mates when they are in possession.

- Impart high-quality information.

- Make good decisions.

- Take positive action.

- Inspire colleagues with confidence.

Over half of the goals scored result from set plays

Given that so many goals are conceded from set pieces, the simplest solution is to avoid giving any away in the defensive third of the field! Since this is unlikely, it is essential that teams develop effective strategies for defending against throw-ins, corners and free kicks. There are three elements that underpin successful defence in these situations.

Preparation and organisation

All teams should rehearse in training the agreed procedure when a set piece is conceded To leave the organisation to chance may result in confusion and hand the initiative to the opposition. Since the idea is to prevent the opposition from exploiting the set piece, all players should know beforehand how the team will respond in a given situation. This will entail instructing certain players to fulfil specific conditions.

Individual responsibility

The best-laid plans will be rendered useless unless individual players carry out the jobs to which they have been assigned. On those occasions when team organisation may be weakened (following a substitution for example), it is important that another player takes responsibility for filling the breach in the defensive formation.

Concentration

Lapses of concentration can prove disastrous even before the ball is delivered. As soon as the set play is conceded, the team should take up their defensive positions. Trigger phrases such as 'When the ball is dead, be alive' will help players to keep on their toes.

The defensive organisation at set plays should be carefully thought out with the appropriate players chosen for the various jobs. It should also be constantly drilled during training sessions with reinforcement given before each game. Some coaches use diagrams stuck to the dressing room wall as a means of reminding the players of their responsibilities. When the opposition's strengths and weaknesses are known to the coach, he may choose to amend the set piece organisation to counteract a specific threat. However, it is usually a good idea to give players regular jobs because this will enhance concentration.

DEFENDING THROW-INS

The short throw

As the ball is being retrieved, the defenders should move quickly into defensive positions. Opponents who constitute the greatest threat should be marked first. Each defender in the vicinity of the throw should mark goalside at a distance of 2–3 yards, forming a triangle between himself, the opponent and the ball. In this position he will be able to cover a sharp movement by his opponent and also make up ground to challenge should the ball be thrown to his attacker. When the opponent receives the ball the defender should put him under heavy pressure to make control difficult and to prevent him from turning. In addition, another defender should be deployed in the space between the nearest attacker and the ball, so that high-quality service back to the thrower is denied and so that the thrower is marked once he enters the field of play. (See Figure 39.)

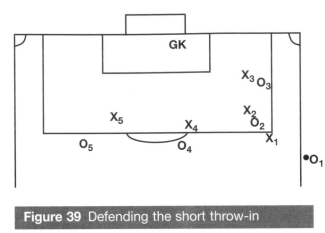

Figure 39 Defending the short throw-in

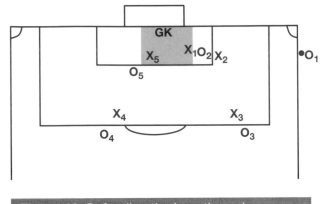

Figure 40 Defending the long throw-in

Defenders well away from the action do not have to mark so tightly since they have a responsibility for covering team-mates as well as looking after their opponent. The goalkeeper should be in the front half of the goal.

The long throw

The long throw can be quite a potent weapon because the trajectory of the ball is usually fairly low and does not allow the keeper much time to deal with it. Defenders can anticipate that opponents are preparing to use the long throw tactic because they usually position a tall target player in the area between the near post and the junction of the 6-yard box. Rather than heading directly for goal, this player will be aiming to get a slight touch on the ball for team-mates in the space behind him. Once the ball has been flicked on, the defence has a problem.

Defensive arrangements should be made to reduce the potency of the throw and to prevent the target player gaining the vital first touch. A defender should stand in front of the thrower to force him to steepen the trajectory of the throw. The higher the trajectory, the longer the ball will be in the air and the more time the defence has to deal with the situation. The normal marking organisation should apply, with the exception of marking in front and behind the opponents' target player. Where possible defenders should mark according to size.

If the attacker does make the flick-on, the defence should then deal with the 'second ball'. The ball is likely to travel 2–6 yards behind the target player.

(See shaded area in Figure 40.) Defenders should be ready to cover this area to prevent any secondary chances.

The high, full-length throw might afford time for the keeper to deal with the first ball. However, if the delivery is shorter and lower with the area in front of the near post congested, the keeper should resist the temptation to attack and deal with the flick-on instead.

DEFENDING CORNERS

There are two basic tactics employed in defending corners: man-to-man or zonal marking. A combination of the two is preferable, because it not only delegates specific areas of responsibility to defenders and the goalkeeper, but also provides the opportunity to cover the opposition's most dangerous players. However, it must be stressed that, as in many cases, the end has to justify the means, and if a team has a system for defending corners that is consistently successful, then they should not tamper with it. It is essential that all players are comfortable with the agreed organisation and, more importantly, believe in it.

The purpose of set piece defensive planning is to make it as difficult as possible for the opposition to score, so it is vital that the team is well drilled and briefed on not only their individual responsibilities, but on the general organisation. There will be occasions in matches when, due to substitutions, key players will be missing and those players remaining on the field of play will have to display the presence

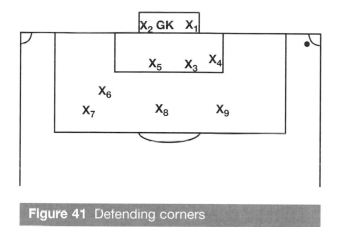

Figure 41 Defending corners

of mind to plug the gaps. This speed of thought may also be required when players are 'dragged' out of position by the movement of opponents.

The corner played into the near post is the most difficult to defend, so it is important that this area is well manned. (See Figure 41.) One player (X1) covers the near post while two other defenders (X3 and X4) mark the space in front of the 6-yard box. Other defenders are stationed at the back post (X2) and at the rear of the 6-yard box (X5). The three players marking the 6-yard box are responsible for the space in front of them and it is important that they are fairly tall and good headers of the ball. The goalkeeper takes care of high balls delivered into the 6-yard box and the two defenders on the post cover the keeper when he leaves his line. Two of the team's smaller players should guard the area between the 6-yard box and the edge of the penalty area to mop up partial clearances. The remaining players should be asked to mark according to size.

It is a good idea to leave at least two of the team's best headers (X6 and X7) to pick up the opposition's dangermen. If the opponents play a short corner, it is important that the zonal markers resist moving out of position and leave the task of pressurising the kick to the shorter players who are marking towards the edge of the box. If, in an emergency, any of the zonal players is to be drawn out of position, it should be the defender guarding the near post because his role is not as critical as those patrolling the front of the 6-yard box. It must also be remembered that when the short corner is played, it requires two defenders to counter it.

When opponents take up positions for a near post corner, it is crucial that defenders mark in front of the first player and behind the last. The object of the exercise is to prevent the ball from being flicked on. This situation presents some difficult decision-making for the keeper – should he attack the corner and risk being beaten by the flick-on, or does he allow the defenders to deal with it and intercept the flick-on if it occurs?

Generally speaking, if the trajectory is flat and defenders are best placed to clear the danger, the keeper should maintain his mid-goal position and prepare to deal with the second ball. On the other hand, if the corner is flighted without much pace and is above the heads of the crowd at the near post, he may have sufficient space and time to claim the ball. In this case experience is the best teacher, but the keeper will be well advised to treat each situation on its own merits and not to commit himself until he has assessed the flight and pace of the ball.

If the opposition sends players deep into the 6-yard box, the keeper should not allow his own players to mark them. To do so would congest his area even further. The keeper must back his ability to beat opponents in the air, if not with a catch then at least with a punch. The zonal markers will deal with the danger if the opponent pulls off the line and out of the 6-yard box. One advantage of zonal marking is that by delegating areas of responsibility, decision making becomes easier. Moreover, the further the opposition is from goal when they meet the ball, the less chance there is of a goal being conceded.

DEFENDING FREE KICKS AROUND THE PENALTY AREA

Free kicks conceded in and around the penalty area will necessitate forming a defensive wall to cover the part of the goal nearest to the ball. Guided by the defensive principle of making play predictable, the wall discourages opponents from shooting directly at the nearest part of the goal. The goalkeeper, who should be positioned in the half of the goal not masked by the wall (so that he can see the ball), will happily deal with shots aimed in his direction because he is only covering part of the goal. (See photo 65.)

Photo 65

As soon as a free kick is awarded the keeper has to decide upon the following:

- Is a wall required?

- Where should it be positioned?

- How many players should be in it?

- Is a charger required?

The number of players in the wall is determined by the position of the free kick. (See Figure 42.) Generally speaking, the nearer and more central the free kick, the greater the number of players in the wall. As the distance of the free kick from the goal increases, the number of players in the wall decreases. Excessive numbers should not be used in the wall as it reduces the number of players available to carry out marking jobs, and it gives the keeper less chance to see the ball.

All teams should have a defensive plan for dealing with free kicks. It is useful to give players positions in the wall. As defenders are usually more adept in marking, the wall is best left to designated midfield players.

As soon as the free kick is awarded, the keeper should organise his defence according to its rehearsed strategy. Skilful players will attempt to take the kick while the keeper is preoccupied with lining up the wall, so it is vitally important that the organisation is slick and takes as little time as possible. (Allowing outfield players to line up the wall requires considerable skill so it is recommended that the keeper, who is obviously in a better position to do so, takes that responsibility.)

The goalkeeper points out which side the wall should cover and decides on the number of players in it. It is best to have the tallest player at the near post side in order to prevent the kicker dipping the ball over the end of the wall. The keeper lines up his end player with the near post and then instructs him to take a step sideways in order to prevent a shot being swerved around the edge of the wall. Instructions should be clear and concise, for instance 'Move two yards to the right. Stop!'. It is imperative that the goalkeeper does not stand behind the wall and thus obscure his view of the ball. With this arrangement, the keeper can prepare himself to receive a direct shot in his half of the goal. If the ball is chipped over or swerved around the wall it will not be hit with pace and, therefore, will give the keeper time to move across and save. The keeper should not gamble and move forward before the ball is struck. Too many goals are scored because the keeper, in anticipating a shot over or around the wall, has moved early and been beaten in the part of the goal he was supposed to be covering. It must be remembered that brilliant creative play will overcome the best defensive strategy so, if the keeper is beaten by an outstanding strike, he should not be blamed if the organisation was as good as it could be.

Occasionally, the kicker will tap the ball inside to increase the shooting angle for another player. To counter this there should be a defensive 'charger' a yard or so off the end of the wall, who will quickly pressurise the ball if it is played sideways. (See X5 in Figure 43.) The keeper should adjust his position accordingly when the ball is played sideways. Other defenders should be used to mark opponents elsewhere in the area.

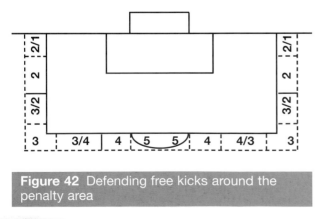

Figure 42 Defending free kicks around the penalty area

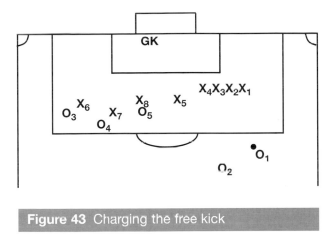

Figure 43 Charging the free kick

For free kicks in wider positions, the wall will not only prevent a direct shot but will also deny the kicker the opportunity to drive in a low cross. As the player will be forced to loft the ball the keeper can tke up a position to defend the cross. The increased height on the ball will give the defence more time to clear the danger.

For those indirect free kicks conceded inside the area, it may be necessary to pull all players back to defend. If the kick is awarded within 10 yards of the goal, it is advisable to have a six- or seven-player wall with the keeper in the middle. As soon as the kick is taken the wall should converge on the ball with the intention of blocking the shot. Spare defenders should be used to mark opponents in the penalty area. (See Figure 44.)

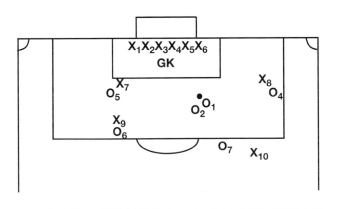

Figure 44 Defending free kicks inside the penalty area

Practices for defending throw-ins, corners and free kicks

These practices can take place in attack v defence situations or in an 11-a-side game. The coach can either wait until throw-ins, corners and free kicks occur naturally, or award them arbitrarily throughout the game.

Key points

- Alertness when the set piece has been conceded. Take up defensive positions as the ball is being retrieved.

- Rapid and calm organisation.

- Awareness of individual and collective responsibilities.

When the value of set piece organisation has been proved in training and reinforced by the coach, players will react automatically in real match situations.

SAVING PENALTIES 15

With the results of so many matches, even World Cup Finals, being decided on penalties, the technique of saving them has assumed greater significance in the modern game

As in one-against-one situations, the pressure during penalty kicks is on the player and not the goalkeeper since, once the ball is placed on the spot, a goal is the expected outcome. Furthermore, during penalty shoot-outs the stress on the penalty taker is even greater, especially when the scores are close. This is particularly true for those players who are not the regular penalty taker. For this reason the keeper might wish to adopt different strategies to suit the situation.

There are two basic techniques: gambling by moving early, or standing up to react to the shot.

MOVING EARLY

The reason why the goalkeeper moves early is because a shot aimed into the corner with pace will otherwise be impossible to save. There are a number of ploys that the keeper can use to assist this guesswork.

Assessing the type of player taking the kick

Generally speaking, defenders take fewer risks than midfield or forward players and tend to play safe by pushing the ball to the same side as the kicking foot. Tricky, skilful players may try to fool the goalkeeper by clipping the ball to the opposite side of the kicking foot.

Trying to 'dummy' the kicker

As the player runs up to take the kick, the keeper feints to move in one direction. The object is to make the kicker think that the keeper is going to dive that way. As a result he places the ball on the other side – right into the arms of the keeper.

Moving backwards and forwards along the goal line

By moving to and fro along the goal line the keeper may put the player off and cause him to misdirect the shot. However, it must be remembered that it is very difficult to dive in one direction while moving in the other!

Standing on one side of the goal

Standing slightly to one side of the centre of the goal may also disrupt the concentration of the kicker who may be forced to change his original intention. It is a brave player who will elect to direct the shot towards the smaller part of the goal. So the goalkeeper should gamble and move to cover the bigger gap.

Observing the approach of the kicker

The run-up of the kicker can give some idea of his body position as he strikes the ball and, therefore, an indication of its intended destination. (See Figure 45.) If the player addresses the ball from a head-on and a very straight approach (A), then it is highly unlikely that he will be able to play the ball to the same side as the kicking foot. The shot will either be delivered straight or swung across the body into the opposite corner. If the approach is curved (B), the kicker is likely to shoot to the same side as the kicking foot. From an angled but fairly straight run-up (C), the shot is likely to be placed back across the keeper.

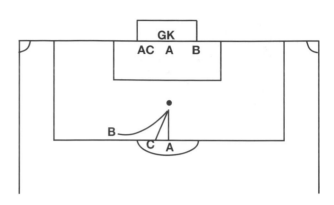

Figure 45 Saving penalties (from a right-footed kicker), observing the approach of the kicker

REACTING TO THE SHOT

During normal play it is likely that the keeper will face the regular penalty taker who will probably have a tried-and-tested approach and sufficient composure to execute an accurate shot. However, in the shoot-out as the pressure mounts, the taker may lose his nerve and his aim. Indeed, personal research of many penalty shoot-out situations has indicated that the majority of shots are played towards the centre of the goal. The keeper should play the percentages and concentrate on defending the middle 6 yards of the goal; the temptation to dive early should be resisted in favour of reacting to the shot. (See Figure 46.)

Whatever saving method is used, it would be unrealistic to expect success every time. Experience will indicate which is the most effective strategy and the keeper should persevere with it. The goalkeeper should, of course, practise the various saving methods, but it is difficult to recreate the tension of real match situations during training sessions since the penalty takers will be fairly relaxed in their approach and be therefore more prepared to take risks.

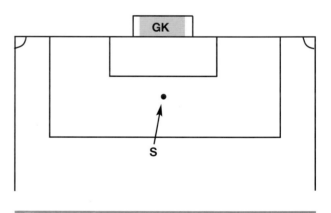

Figure 46 Saving penalties – reacting to the shot, defending the middle 6 yards

FITNESS TRAINING 16

The demands of the modern game necessitate specific physical conditioning for the goalkeeper

Fitness training, like coaching, is a means to an end. Unless it results in improving match performance, it is pointless. Players who wish to fulfil their potential must ensure that they are fully equipped to meet the demands of the modern game. To put it another way, players should not be able to blame poor preparation for a sub-standard performance. The importance of a comprehensive coaching programme and pre-match warm-up has already been discussed, but this will be negated if players are not physically capable of sustaining a desirable level of performance. Consequently, the coach should be aware of the fitness needs of all of his players.

Reaching peak fitness and then maintaining it is not easy and it is not without its share of discomfort. There is a saying, 'No pain, no gain', which contains a large element of truth. Players must work hard in training throughout the season because fitness is not like a bank account that accrues interest when left alone. It must be constantly topped up or the level will diminish. The key to maintaining fitness is motivation. If training is enjoyable, purposeful and competitive, players will be motivated to push themselves so that fitness benefits result.

Since fitness is so important, the coach must not approach the subject haphazardly. The whole programme should be carefully planned. Below are the key points.

- The identification of training needs which relate to the age and performance level of the players involved.

- The timing of the fitness programme. It is likely that the most intensive work will take place during the pre-season training period. Subsequent fitness sessions throughout the year will be aimed at maintaining levels. Care should be taken that intensive work does not take place too close to matches because performance may be impaired.

- The implementation of a varied training programme based on quality rather than quantity of work.

- The regular, objective monitoring of fitness during training sessions. This can be achieved reliably via time trials, circuit training, etc.

- The regular, subjective evaluation of fitness levels during matches.

Goalkeepers require an all-round fitness. They need to have quick feet and good spring, but also the upper body strength to cope with the hardest of shots and the strongest of physical challenges. In addition, they ought to possess the suppleness and speed of reaction to deal with the unexpected. All of these qualities need to be founded upon a good level of cardio-vascular fitness.

In order to make the work realistic and enjoyable a ball should be used as much as possible. However, it is imperative that the coach appreciates the difference between coaching and training. Many people wrongly assume that goalkeeping coaching is pressure training (rapid repetitions of a particular exercise). Skill levels will break down once fatigue sets in, so when coaching a particular technique, the keeper needs time to digest the key factors if he is to carry out the practice successfully. With pressure training, there is little time for such reflection and within a few minutes the player is too exhausted to perform the technique in the desired manner. Pressure training has its uses in improving endurance and strength, but not in the perfection of technique.

Coaches must ensure that the training is appropriate for the players involved. For younger players the emphasis should be on enjoyment and the mastery of technique with any fitness benefits being incidental. However, for goalkeepers working at the elite level it is recommended that supervised basic strength training and conditioning should commence from the age of 12 years. As players mature physically the specific fitness demands (including degree of difficulty, number of sets and repetitions) will increase. There are many excellent fitness specific books on the market that will provide a more comprehensive range of exercises than this one. This chapter will cover drills that require minimal equipment and are relatively easy to organise.

Four fitness areas for goalkeepers are identified and a selection of exercises for each is provided below. As the list is by no means exhaustive the coach should use his imagination to keep the sessions varied and fresh. **It is recommended that, with the exception of speed work, fitness drills occur towards the end of sessions once the technical/tactical aspects have been covered**.

ENDURANCE

The goalkeeper should not be excused from running drills involving outfield players, but there are some activities which are specific to his position.

(1) THE BARRAGE
Organisation
A number of balls are spread out in an arc around the goal-mouth (10 yards from the goal line). Starting at one end, the server shoots in rapid succession. The keeper has to save as many shots as possible. (See Figure 47.) After a brief rest (3:1 rest to work ratio) the exercise is repeated with the keeper trying to improve his previous score. The server may wish to vary the distance of the shots depending on the goalkeeper's needs. It is vitally important that the service is tailored to the ability of the keeper. Sufficient time between each shot must be allowed so that good technique is maintained throughout. In other words, the keeper must be given the chance to save. Merely blasting every shot into the back of the net will demotivate the keeper and afford very little benefit.

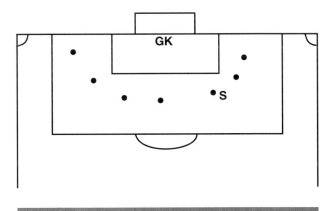

Figure 47 The barrage

(2) THE CORRIGAN

Organisation

This exercise is named after the former Manchester City and England goalkeeper Joe Corrigan, who included it as part of his daily training routine. Two servers stand level with a post 6–7 yards from the goal, armed with four balls each. One server feeds the ball low towards the post so that the keeper is forced to make a diving save. As he gets up, the second server feeds high towards the other post. The keeper has to move quickly to save. This process is repeated until all the balls have been used. This exercise is extremely demanding and the goalkeeper should be given sufficient rest before repeating it. For more advanced performers, the number of balls can be increased. (See photos 66a, 66b, 66c, 66d, 66e, 66f and 66g.)

Photo 66d

Photo 66e

Photo 66a

Photo 66f

Photo 66b

Photo 66g

Photo 66c

(3) THE SHUTTLE
Organisation
This exercise involves three goals – two 5-yard goals located 15 yards from the goal line on each side of the goal, and a full-size goal. (See Figure 48.) The keeper, starting from his near post, approaches goal A and server 1(S1) forces him to make a sharp save. The keeper has to recover immediately and look to save from S2 shooting at goal B. He then touches the far post and approaches goal C to make another sharp save from S3. The keeper has one final shot to save from S2 aiming for goal B. The exercise is repeated five times (with 3:1 rest to work ratios) and is conducted at high speed.

(4) THE CIRCUIT
Organisation
The goalkeeper sprints 12 yards to two balls placed 1 yard apart. He completes 15 press-ups with his hands on top of the balls. He sprints back to the start, completes a forward roll, turns and sprints out to another ball 15 yards from the line. The keeper dives flat on to his stomach and the coach throws the ball into the air. The keeper has to leap to his feet and catch the ball at the highest point possible. This is repeated 10 times. He then sprints back to the line, completes a forward roll, turns and sprints

out to another ball 18 yards away. Here the goalkeeper lies flat on his back and the server throws the ball so that the keeper has to sit up to catch. This is repeated 30 times. The keeper sprints back to the line, completes a forward roll and then rests. Advanced performers can attempt two or three circuits without rest. Younger players can complete each circuit with a 3:1 rest to work ratio in between. (See Figure 49.) In order to monitor progress, the coach could record the time taken to complete the circuit(s).

(5) CONTINUOUS COLLAPSING SAVES
Organisation
The keeper starts at one end of the goal area with server standing 4–6 yards away. The server plays the ball along the ground forcing the goalkeeper to make a collapsing save. Having made the save, the keeper rolls the ball back as he gets to his feet. The server returns the ball so that the goalkeeper makes another collapsing save. This process continues until the other end of the goal area is reached at which point the exercise continues in the opposite direction. Three return journeys are completed before resting. The server must control the pace of the practice so that the keeper has sufficient time to perform the save correctly.

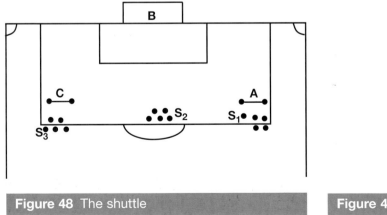

Figure 48 The shuttle

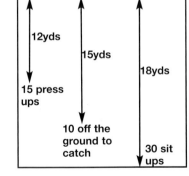

Figure 49 The circuit

SPEED/REACTION TIME

When engaged in speed training it is very imporant that the goalkeeper works at maximal effort and is allowed to fully recover between exercises.

(1) SQUARE SPRINTING
Organisation
The goalkeeper starts in the middle of a 10 yard square with balls placed in each corner. On the command he sprints out to the corner, touches the ball, turns, returns to the middle, touches the ball and then moves off to another corner. This process is repeated until each ball has been touched. Rest to work ratios should be at least 5:1. On subsequent exercises the type of running required can be varied, for example, forward out and backwards back to the middle, or sideways out and sideways back. (See photo 67.)

Photo 67

(2) SHORT SPRINTING
Organisation
This exercise is best conducted with two or more players performing at the same time to create a competitive situation. The keeper lies or sits 5 yards from the ball. On the command he has to rise and gather the ball as quickly as possible. The coach may vary the starting position and the distance to be covered. Once again the rest to work ratio should be 5:1.

(3) OFF THE GROUND TO SAVE
Organisation
The goalkeeper lies or kneels 12 yards from the goal line facing his own goal. The server standing 5–10 yards away at an angle plays the ball towards goal. On the command from the server the keeper has to rise and move quickly to prevent the ball from crossing the line (see Figure 50).

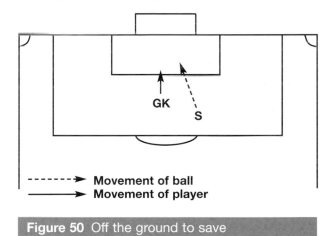

- - - - - - ▶ **Movement of ball**
—————▶ **Movement of player**

Figure 50 Off the ground to save

(4) QUICK PICK-UPS
Organisation
The keeper stands at one end of a 10 yard grid. The server throws the ball into the grid and the keeper has to pick it up before the second bounce (see Figure 51).

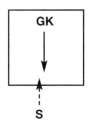

Figure 51 Quick pick-ups

AGILITY/FLEXIBILITY

This section should be considered along with the stretching exercises on page 11 as they can be used to improve flexibility if held for longer.

(1) FORWARD ROLL
Organisation
With the ball in his hands, the goalkeeper completes a forward roll and returns to the feet in one movement. The exercise is repeated 6 times.

(2) LOWER BACK FLEXIBILITY
Organisation
The goalkeeper lies flat on his stomach and the server feeds the ball from a distance of 1–2 yards so that the keeper is forced to arch his back to make the catch. The exercise is repeated 10 times. (See photo 68.)

(3) GLIDING ON THE BACKSIDE
Organisation
The goalkeeper sits on the floor and the server feeds the ball to alternate sides. After each save the goalkeeper must thrust himself forwards without using his hands. Rhythmic feeding by the server will help the keeper move his trunk from the goal line to the edge of the penalty area.

(4) AVOIDING THE BALL
Organisation
The goalkeeper lies on his back with the servers 3 yards either side of him. One server rolls the ball towards the keeper who has to take evasive action so that it carries on unimpeded to the other server. The keeper can let the ball pass through by sitting up, arching his back or lifting his legs. The exercise is repeated 20 times. (See photos 69a and 69b.)

Photo 68

Photo 69a

Photo 69b

STRENGTH

(1) SPRING EXERCISES
Organisation
Using a series of five hurdles or balls, the goalkeeper has to bounce over each obstacle. The keeper should use a variety of take-offs – bunny hops, left-leg hops, and right-leg hops. He should aim to achieve maximum spring over each obstacle. Care should be taken that the surface is not too hard to prevent joint injuries. There should be plenty of rest between each set. (See photo 70.)

Photo 70

(2) OFF THE GROUND AND SPRING
Organisation
The keeper takes a variety of positions on the ground. On the command the server throws the ball into the air and the goalkeeper has to rise quickly and jump to catch it. Repeat 10 times. In order to develop greater spring the keeper should be encouraged not to use the hands when getting up from his back or side.

(3) RISE TO BACK PEDAL TO SAVE
Organisation
The keeper sits on the six yard line with the sever standing on the penalty spot. On the command the server throws the ball towards the goal. The keeper has to rise without the help of his hands, back pedal quickly and jump to catch the ball. Repeat 10 times.

(4) ABDOMINAL EXERCISES
Organisation
There are a number of exercises that can be used to develop abdominal strength.

a) Sitting on the ground the goalkeeper has to catch balls delivered rapidly to alternate sides by the server standing 2–3 yards away. 20 serves to each side.

b) Sitting on the ground, with his knees bent, the goalkeeper lies with the ball in his hands. He lifts his lower back from the ground to touch his knees with the ball. Repeat 20 times.

c) As in b) but as he rises the keeper twists his trunk to touch the ball on the outside of his right knee. In the next sit-up he touches the outside of his left knee. 10 repetitions for each side.

d) The keeper lies on his back with a ball resting on one hand. With his knees bent he slowly lifts his lower back from the ground. Hold for 5–10 seconds before slowly lowering to the ground. Repeat 5 times with the ball in each hand. Progress to raising the right leg when the ball is in the right hand. Repeat for the left side.

(5) PRESS-UPS

A choice of one of the following should be carried out at least three times per week.

- Ordinary press-ups (3 x 25).

- Press-ups on the knuckles (3 x 25).

- Press-ups on the fingers (3 x 15).

- Press-ups on two balls (3 x 10). (See photo 71.)

- Press-ups on one ball (3 x 10). (See photo 72.)

- 1 press-up, clap hands; 2 press-ups, clap hands; 3 press-ups, clap hands, and so on up to 10 press-ups.

- Press-up with one hand on the ball and one hand on the ground. After each press-up shift the ball to the other hand and repeat (3 x 10).

Obviously, the number of press-ups will relate to the age and level of the performer, but the volume should increase over time.

Photo 71

Photo 72

The health and safety of the players should be the coach's responsibility

Whilst it is acknowledged that there have been some tremendous recent technological advances in producing artificial surfaces with all the characteristics of natural turf, the vast majority of coaches have access only to the traditional sand filled or water based pitches. This chapter is written with the latter's needs in mind. Goalkeepers require access to grass facilities more than any other players. While artificial surfaces can assist outfield players to perfect their passing and control, they can pose long-term dangers for goalkeepers who constantly throw themselves about on them. It is not in the young goalkeeper's interest to engage in excessive long-diving on hard surfaces. Not only can the constant pounding lead to overuse injuries, there is also the possibility that the keeper might develop incorrect techniques as a means of protecting himself. As young goalkeepers are often keen to impress and generally know no fear, it is important that the coach is aware of the potential dangers and that he exercises some control when organising coaching sessions.

It is inevitable that goalkeepers will dive during training sessions on artificial surfaces, but by restricting the intensity and the length of the dives, the coach will succeed in limiting potential injuries. Protective clothing in the form of elbow pads and padded training bottoms will reduce the incidence of bruising and abrasions. The simplest device the coach can use to restrict the amount of long-diving is to use markers to make small goals. Most of the practices included in this book can be adapted so that the goalkeeper does not have to go to ground too often.

The other main constraint inherent in working on artificial surfaces, particularly indoors, is space. Here the coach will have to demonstrate flexibility in his organisation and by liaising closely with others sharing the facility, he should be able to attain his coaching objectives without sacrificing safety concerns or quality of practice.

When planning a long-term programme, the coach can work to a cyclical syllabus based on the following.

- Ball familiarity – no restrictions.
- Dealing with the back pass – no restrictions.
- Handling: the four hand shapes – restricted to diving from the kneeling position.
- Footwork exercises – no restrictions except no diving.
- Shot-stopping – defending small goal only.
- Imperfect world – defending small goal only.
- Positioning – handball game with no diving.
- Diving at feet – from kneeling position.
- Reaction work – rebound work from a wall into a small goal is very useful.
- The high cross – no restrictions.
- Distribution – no restrictions.
- Supporting the defence – no restrictions.
- Organisation of set pieces – no restrictions.
- Penalties – theory only.

When the opportunity to work on grass surfaces presents itself, the coach should seize it and seek to consolidate the work covered on a regular basis in a more realistic environment.

The name of the game is keeping the ball out of the net

The aim of goalkeeping is to keep the ball out of the net, and if the keeper manages to do this safely and consistently using unorthodox techniques, his 'style' must not be coached out of him. The purpose of this handbook is to help the goalkeeper carry out his job effectively, not to attain marks for artistic merit. So, if a keeper's method is successful game after game, the coach should not attempt to change it. My advice to youngsters is to observe and appreciate the top goalkeepers, but be wary of imitating them. Young players should develop their own style based on an awareness of their own strengths and limitations.

It is irritating when people discount promising young goalkeepers because they are 'too small'. Teenagers grow at different rates and a below average sized goalkeeper at 11 years of age may be considerably taller than his peers by the age of 18. Furthermore, all keepers have their strengths and weaknesses and a short player's strong points might be a taller player's failings. If the goalkeeper is performing well, making few errors, his height will not be an important factor. Since the coach can do little about genetics, he should concentrate on helping his promising young players to fulfil their potential.

On the subject of physique, it would appear that over the last ten years the average height of goalkeepers at the highest level has risen from about 6' 1" to 6' 3". There is a well known cliché in soccer that 'A big good 'un is always better than a small good 'un', and this is true for goalkeeping positions where the physical demands of the game can be very intense.

Notwithstanding physique, in an attempt to determine what makes a good goalkeeper, ten interdependent key areas, the ten Cs, have been identified.

CONFIDENCE

Confidence is the foundation on which all other aspects of goalkeeping are built. Without it the keeper will not approach the job in a positive manner, performances will become erratic, and his team will suffer because of his unreliability. In the goalkeeping context, confidence is an unfailing belief in one's ability, despite the occasional set-back. Inevitably mistakes will be made, but the good player puts them at the back of his mind and continues unaffected for the rest of the game. The uncertain keeper fails to come to terms with his errors and, doubting his ability, fails to perform to his full potential. What he must remember is that one mistake does not mean that he has suddenly become a poor player. Indeed, a more accurate indicator of his worth can be observed in his response after the error has been make. In short, the only thing that the goalkeeper has to fear is fear itself.

A goalkeeper should never show that he is frightened because that hands the initiative to the opposition. Even if he feels nervous he should give the impression of being in total control both of himself and his fellow defenders. Such a display will inspire self-belief and the confidence of those around him.

During those off-form periods when the goalkeeper feels confidence draining away, he should recall games in which he has performed well and re-live them repeatedly in his mind. By visualising these memories, the keeper will build up a positive picture of himself and his abilities. This re-kindled self-esteem will help to dissipate the fear and negative attitude caused by a loss of form. It is at these times that the coach can play a vital role in maintaining the keeper's self-belief. Constant encouragement combined with appropriate coaching practice will accelerate the return to peak performance.

COMPETENCE

All players should work conscientiously at improving their skill level. This will entail polishing their strong points until they catch the eye, and working hard to rectify weaknesses.

The goalkeeper's training schedule should revolve around reducing the number of mistakes made during matches. As mistakes are caused by technical errors or wrong decisions, it should be fairly easy to identify where problems are occurring. Training sessions should be spent concentrating on those areas causing the keeper concern so that he has the opportunity to correct any faults appearing in his game. However, he should still devote some time to working on the fundamental areas of head, hands and feet, because mastery of the basics will make the difficult saves look easy.

Although there is no substitute for match experience in assisting the learning process, the training sessions should stretch the keeper so that a high level of skill and commitment is demanded. Good habits in training will spread to match performance and, as competence grows, the keeper will radiate confidence.

CONCENTRATION

It only takes a split-second to let in a goal, so if the keeper 'switches off' during a game, the result could be disastrous. He must live every second of the game and be ready for any eventuality. Unlike outfield players, the keeper cannot go off in pursuit of the ball, searching for action. The extent to which he is occupied depends on how successful the opposition is in getting the ball close to his goal.

Generally speaking, it is easier to perform effectively when constantly involved in the action rather than when called upon to make a save only once in a while. When inactive for long spells, it is essential that the goalkeeper maintains a high level of concentration and tries to involve himself in the game as much as possible. Even when play is in the opponent's half he can be constantly adjusting his position ready for a quick breakaway and, of course, he can keep in touch with play by being a source of information and encouragement for the defenders in front of him.

The key to good concentration is taking nothing for granted and being primed for action at all times. This means treating every shot with respect and being prepared for the worst from team-mates and the best from opponents.

COMPETITIVENESS

All goalkeepers should be determined not to be beaten, and if they are, it should be a momentary personal tragedy. Unless the keeper is prepared to fully commit himself (including risking personal safety) in order to prevent a goal, he will never be successful. A strong competitive streak will result in a positive approach to the game and will boost confidence. Indeed, the manner in which a keeper performs is just as important as his physical characteristics. If the goalkeeper believes he is a giant who has to dominate his area, he will play like one, irrespective of size. Like confidence, this will to win is infectious and a keeper can inspire his defenders with the same determination to keep his goal intact.

It is important that players are also competitive in training because it is not a quality that can be turned on like a tap just for matches. The determination not to concede a goal must be a permanent feature of the keeper's make-up. This committment to wining will result in a conscientious approach to training and will ensure that areas of weakness are given sufficient attention.

COMPOSURE

The ability to keep your head when everyone else is losing their's is a vital quality, since the goalkeeping position is a highly pressurised one. As the linchpin of the defence, the keeper cannot allow himself to panic when under stress. Other players will look to him to set the tone so it is important that he exudes a calm authority. Goalkeepers who constantly harangue the defence run the risk of losing concentration and alienating colleagues. There is a place for the justified reprimand, but it should be employed sparingly.

CONSISTENCY

One of the qualities that top goalkeepers possess is the ability to perform to a high standard game after game. Keepers who have proved their reliability over a number of matches will be greatly valued by their teams. Being consistent entails carrying out the job efficiently with very few costly mistakes.

The key to consistency is the relentless application of the basics coupled with good decision-making in every game, whatever the prevailing conditions or quality of opposition. This requires considerable powers of concentration because there will be days when the keeper feels below par and his mind starts wandering. He must prevent this by harnessing his competitive instincts in such a way that all he thinks about during the game is keeping the ball out of the net. Good preparation can enhance concentration so that the mind and body are tuned in, ready to make a save as soon as the game starts.

The enemy of consistency is complacency. The moment that the keeper starts taking the game for granted, he will be embarrassed. He must treat every game and every situation in the same respectful way. Complacency breeds sloppiness which, in turn, leads to mistakes. From the time that he arrives at the ground until the end of the match, the keeper should devote his mind and energies to keeping the ball out of the net.

COURAGE

There are bound to be occasions during matches when the keeper, in an attempt to prevent a goal, risks injury. These situations demand raw courage inspired by the desire not to be beaten. However, if the keeper applies the correct technique and commits himself fully to the physical confrontation, serious injury should seldom result. In any case, most keepers feel more pain when the ball hits the back of the net than when personally taking a physical knock. Often the keeper's courage can turn a game, especially in 1 v 1 situations.

Courage of a different sort is the mental strength to make crucial decisions. For instance, when conditions are muddy and the opposition aggressive, it is easier to stay on the line than to come for a high cross. However, the keeper has to back his ability and make the correct decision. This mental courage will be tested to the full during those times when confidence is low and negative tendencies predominate over the positive. Form will only be rediscovered by conquering fear and making the correct decisions.

CO-OPERATION

In the modern game, the goalkeeper is more than a saver of shots and fielder of crosses. He is now expected to play as an extra defender patrolling the area behind the defence. A feature of all good defences is compactness and this can only be achieved if the distance between the keeper and the rearmost defender does not become too great. This will require a degree of soccer intelligence on the part of the keeper who will need to take up sensible supporting positions backed by clear, early information.

COMMUNICATION

As the last line of defence, the goalkeeper is perfectly placed to view the whole game as it unfolds in front of him. Consequently, he should be a constant source of information and encouragement for his team. Through effective use of his voice, he can make his team-mates aware of unforeseen dangers and ensure that the defence is well organised. For this reason it is important that the goalkeeper knows when, what, and how to communicate.

A clear, early call can result in a blind-side run being picked up or it can help a defender decide upon a course of action when under pressure. Given in the correct manner and at the appropriate time, intelligent information can nip potentially dangerous situations in the bud. This ability to communicate effectively comes with experience which, in turn, is born out of an open-minded and conscientious approach to the game.

COACHING

Coaching is about improving players and helping them to fulfil their potential. If all the afore-mentioned personal attributes are equal, then it will be the quality of coaching that gives a player the edge over his peers. The effective coach will bring out the best in the goalkeeper, nurturing what natural talent he possesses through a well structured training programme. Without such guidance, an individual's development is left to chance and the cultivation of bad habits will remain unchecked.

FINAL ADVICE 19

You're really only as good as the next game

Every goalkeeper, throughout the history of the game, has experienced at some time the utter despair of making mistakes that have cost crucial goals. Sometimes fate conspires to compound this misery so that the error affects the result of the game or even the fortunes of a whole season. The 24 hours immediately after the game are the worst, when the goalkeeper constantly relives the incidents in his mind, longing for the next training session when he can exorcise the memories.

It is comforting to know that even the true greats of the game have visited this lonely place. However, it is how they come to terms with their mistakes that marks them out from the rest. Rather than let one mistake or poor performance damage confidence and herald a run of poor form, they put the mistake down to experience and work hard in training to ensure that it does not happen again. Furthermore, no-one can turn back the clock, we can only deal with the present, and by adopting this philosophy, the keeper should be able to concentrate on the remainder of the match. Unless a goalkeeper can handle the pressure of dealing with mistakes he will never fulfil his potential.

Aside from developing this mental toughness, the goalkeeper owes it to himself and to his team to be in peak physical condition for match play. This will not only involve working hard in training but also approaching the game in the correct manner. All successful keepers have a single-minded determination to keep the ball out of the net. It is this commitment which drives them to practise hard and to perfect their craft. The keeper should also strive to cultivate an on-field personality which gives the impression that he is king of the penalty area and that he has everything under control. This will fuel both himself and his team-mates with confidence.

In training, the keeper should concentrate on polishing technique and improving decision-making. However, he should remember that there are occasions when application of the perfect technique is impossible and an untidy save is the only option. Moreover, the keeper must never lose sight of the fact that his job is to keep the ball out of the net, and if he mishandles a shot, he must make a second save. Many goalkeepers, angry at not making a clean catch, lose concentration after dropping the ball and fail to regain possession immediately. This can, of course, prove disastrous.

The good keeper will become a keen student of the game and be able to quickly analyse situations that develop in front of him. By understanding the roles and responsibilities of team-mates as well as the capabilities of opponents, the goalkeeper will be able to read the game better and to identify and nullify threats before they become a problem.

Above all, the keeper should try to be consistent. It is a useful analogy to equate good performances with deposits in a bank. When the goalkeeper plays well, he makes a deposit, while performing poorly results in a withdrawal. Aiming to reach a pre-determined number of deposits can motivate the keeper to perform well game after game.

Goalkeeping check list

- Constantly practise handling and foot-work skills.

- Work on control with the feet, in every training session.

- Treat every shot with respect.

- Make positive decisions whenever possible.

- Never switch off during games – play every moment.

- Cultivate an on-field personality that takes charge of the penalty area.

- Try to be a good reader of the game.

- Develop good communication with fellow defenders.

- Do not neglect work on distribution skills.

- Be organised at set pieces.

- Prepare correctly for every game.

- Keep physically fit.

- Take good care of equipment.

- Do not dwell on mistakes.

- Always be positive and never lose faith in your ability.

Reminders for the coach

In recognising that the goalkeeper occupies the single most important position in the team, the team coach should ensure that the keeper is given sufficient time in which to practise his craft. Merely completing a training session with a shooting drill will not satisfy a keeper's needs. He should have a personalised coaching programme aimed at polishing his strengths and minimising his weaknesses.

The foundations

All training sessions should incorporate work on the basics of head, hands and feet so that good habits are firmly established. In addition, the coach should be able to identify areas of concern from match play, and should then arrange a session which concent-rates on those aspects. The coaching session should begin at a level where the keeper experiences some success before progressing to increasingly realistic practice situations. This progression from the easy to the difficult will help improve the keeper's confidence as well as his competence.

Good quality service

The feeding of the ball during training sessions is very important because progress will only be made if the keeper has the opportunity to make contact with the ball. The service should be challenging and attempt to bring out the best in the goalkeeper. Indeed, it can be soul destroying to be constantly retrieving the ball from the back of the net.

Outfield practice

With the current Laws concerning the back pass, it is a useful exercise to allow the keeper some outfield practice in small-sided game situations. Moreover, most teams expect their goalkeepers to act as a sweeper and to leave the penalty area to deal with through balls, so regular practice without the hands is recommended.

Boosting morale

It is important that players enjoy their soccer. The coach can encourage this by making training sessions both productive and stimulating. Adhering to the premise that praise is a stronger motivating agent than criticism, the coach should ensure that the keeper leaves the training field confident in his ability and fully prepared for the next match. One way of doing this is to end every session with a save so that the keeper's self-esteem is left intact.

FINALLY

Since the position in which they play is such a pressurised one, goalkeepers find it difficult to enjoy the game while it is in progress. Therefore, the enjoyment tends to be retrospective. It is later on, when he has time to unwind and analyse his performance, that the keeper can look back on the game and his performance with pride or disappointment. Generally speaking, an error-free game provides as much satisfaction as brilliant one-off saves. There is no better feeling than relaxing after a match reflecting upon a job well done.

INDEX